BUILDING LUCRATIVE INCOME WITH AN AIRBNB BUSINESS

THE LOW BUDGET BEGINNER'S GUIDE TO CREATING PASSIVE INCOME WITH VACATION RENTALS

SARAH L. CARTER

CONTENTS

AUTHOR BIO

A long-time North Carolina resident with a passion for the city's distinctive architecture and design, Sarah L. Carter brings more than 14 years of sales experience and a reputation for honesty, trustworthiness, along with superior negotiating skills to the Airbnb agency.

Originally from the South, Sarah moved to New York in 2008 and spent the next two decades as a director of sales and events for some of the most popular restaurants and nightlife around the city. Leveraging her extensive global network and mastering the city's most desirable neighborhoods, she now serves as an invaluable resource to a diverse set of entrepreneurs and travelers across New York State in her Airbnb establishments.

With patience, genuineness, and commitment to her clients, Sarah has served the Airbnb agency as a sales representative for one of the city's most-esteemed, luxury high-rise buildings. Having lived in some of NY's most desirable enclaves from Manhattan to

Westchester Area, she offers her clients invaluable insight into the lifestyle afforded by each neighborhood, along with a keen eye for interior design, and a knack for seeing potential in every property.

Sarah is also a proud mom to her one- and two-year-old daughters. When she's not hosting an Airbnb reservation or searching for the next opportunity to recreate an Airbnb property for clients, she enjoys relaxing at the café and devotes her time and resources to Care Rescue NY and Moses Children's Hospital.

INTRODUCTION

Anyone who is not investing now is missing a tremendous opportunity.

— CARLOS SLIM

Who would have thought that an idea for a quick rent fix would today be a multibillion dollar company? Certainly not the founders of the renowned online marketplace that connects people who have spare home space to rent out and accommodation seekers in different locations across the world. The story of how Airbnb was founded is a fascinating one, yet so relatable, it could have happened to you. Most people think that to partake in vacation rentals they have to be real estate moguls with thick clientele portfolios, the elite with luxury homes in major cities, or anyone belonging to the super wealthy club of investors looking to diversify their portfolios by investing their money offshore or anywhere in the world where wealth seems to be transitioning to.

Prior to this epiphany, hardly did it come to mind that even my ordinary home could bring me income irrespective of whether I had fully paid it off or I was still an active dweller myself. But when Air Bed and Breakfast founders Brian Chesky and Joe Gebbia needed help covering their rent and all they had was three extra air mattresses—hence the name—they took a chance and invited three guests who had come to the designers' conference in their area. They saw a gap as hotels were fully booked for the event and they had space. Then they created a website and used it to make an irresistible accommodation offer. As fate would have it, the guests paid to sleep in the spare living room, enjoyed a well-prepared breakfast together, and had a local experience during their stay. The guests found alternative accommodation at an affordable price compared to the hotels that were fully booked and going for an exorbitant price. Chesky and Gebbia were able to pay that month's rent by simply hosting guests for a few days. As a cherry on top, the guests were treated to sightseeing around the city, and they became friends (Fundersand-founders, 2014).

It's from this experience that Chesky and Gebbia realized that they might have struck gold with this idea and gave it more thought. Having solved their immediate quick cash injection, they wondered how many people would benefit from the same strategy. From this angle of willing to share their strategy to help others, they solved their major problem—limited space to accommodate more guests and making more money. It was mind-blowing to realize that they did not specifically need to own any more homes for their business to scale. All they had to do was build a platform where their key players would meet and find common ground.

Driven by passion and determination, they pitched their idea to locals as well as investors. While some home owners were skeptical to share their most intimate spaces with strangers, others were keen to the idea. To investors, however, this idea was ludicrous and doomed to fail. As designers, Chesky and Gebbie, together with their third roommate, co-founder, and engineer Nathan Blecharcyzk, realized that they can design to build trust between their key players. That's how they constructed a website that has just enough details that makes meeting strangers less scary and more convenient for both the host and the guest.

Competition with existing vacation rentals sites and the behemoth hotel businesses was the least of their worries as they were determined to offer something different to the market. It's possible to be intimidated as one enters the humongous hospitality industry with no experience, property, or capital as an individual. Even I thought, who am I to even consider having a stake in this industry without all three key components to begin with? Lo and behold, through personal success in this niche, the contents of this book are bound to give away the strategies of how to get started in the Airbnb business with minimal investment and make lucrative profits without the need to own property or put down a large sum of capital.

With 14 years' experience in sales and over five years of mentorship in real estate, property investment, and now, Airbnb hosting, I've had my fair share of learning the ins and outs of this business. I've managed to overcome my fears of failure and finally took action to make phenomenal success with this business. It is thus my utmost reason to share my experience to help you also find confidence to start and succeed in this business.

If you've ever wondered how you can rub shoulders with the elite in the property and hospitality industry, this book is a must-read as it outlines how you can be successful and make huge profits from a small investment. Dive deeper to find out the secret to having more freedom to enjoy life with your loved ones as you stumble on the golden strategy on how to scale this business through automation and rental arbitrage. What are you waiting for? Turn that page already and feast on the real gold nuggets reserved for the elite. Welcome to the club!

1

THE AIRBNB UNIVERSE

If you launch and no one notices, launch again. We launched three times.

— BRIAN CHESKY, CEO OF AIRBNB

THE AIRBNB OVERVIEW

What Is an Airbnb?

Founded in 2007, Airbnb is an online marketplace that brings together empty nesters and accommodation seekers in specific locales. This entails people who rent out the spare space in their homes—regardless of whether they own the property or not—to random travelers and guests who are looking for alternative accommodation that is relatively cheaper than a hotel (Folger, 2021). Depending on the type of property, some dwellers either rent out a separate unit with private facilities to guests or they can share the living space with guests in their homes. Usually, the guests that opt for this type of accommodation are looking for something different, more intimate, and homey. With a touch of local experience thrown in the mix, the guests mostly strive to live like locals inside someone's home instead of being in a fancy hotel that turns out to be a bit impersonal.

This is a growing niche in the hospitality business as both the hosts and guests find the middle ground to coexist in one property in a shared economy. Without the hassle of being a licensed hotel business where there is a lot of red tape, owners can simply open their homes and take in strangers who are looking to reserve money from expensive accommodation and fine dining. They achieve this by moving into a place fitted with appliances they are likely to find in their homes, having a new experience, and mixing with the locals so that they don't feel like tourists. To some extent, and varying from one host to another, some homes have facilities and amenities that guests would find in hotels, like welcome gifts, fresh towels, soaps, wine, coffee, or tea, and if requested, room service.

What makes Airbnb unique is that, unlike hotels that have a certain standard to uphold, it can be exciting for guests to experience different homes as reception and amenities differ from what one would expect. This makes the experience something to look forward to in different locations. Similarly, hosts also have something to look forward to as they open their homes to different guests from different places, opening up space for friendships and a flavorful life. That being said, Airbnb is for both adventurous hosts and guests alike, with a way to benefit both to make and save money through a more personalized experience.

How Was Airbnb Created?

A brainchild of three friends and roommates, Brian Chesky, Joe Gebbia, and Nathan Blecharcyzk, this multibillion dollar platform started when Joe Gebbia was broke and his rent had become more expensive for him after his former roommate Nathan had moved to another city. After learning that there was a shortage of accommodation due to the design conference, Gebbia then pitched to his new roommate, Chesky, how he had found a way to make money by inviting paying guests to sleep on their air mattresses and have breakfast during their stay. After their first successful hosting experience, Gebbia and Chesky pitched their idea to investors and other hosts, hoping it would be a smooth sail—and it was an epic fail (TED, 2016).

There were controversies of how risky the business was such that investors wanted no part in it, while hosts that tried out the experience were lacking in training on how to make their listings captivating to clients. The business that looked solid and promising in the beginning started to show walls cracking and fell flat over time. However, there were lessons to be learned and a plot twist to solve cash flow problems while going back to the drawing board to relaunch the business. Determined to get their business off the ground, the founding friends found a way to raise funds by making their breakfast cereal—*Obama O's, hope in every bowl*, and *Cap'n McCain's, a maverick in every bite*—aligning it with and capitalizing on the controversial political era. When the Obama O's sold out in a day, that was a sensational topic and a lasting memory in the Airbnb founding days. The founders reached out to media houses and sent them a box of their cereal. While they initially only made enough to afford buying, repackaging, and selling the cereal, they knocked on doors to make their product a go-to breakfast cereal. Their success was eminent as their cereal became a household brand that eventually turned into a $25 million company, and they knew then that all their hard work had paid off.

From the phenomenon "be a cereal entrepreneur," the Airbnb founders are proof that you can achieve anything if you're determined to think outside the box and be open to take a chance. Thus said, it was not easy to get Airbnb off the ground, but through determination, the founders launched three times before the business could take up space and become a global brand. They learned to do things that did not scale when they visited their clients, helped them to fit the brand, and found ways to support them until they were ready to expand with a redefined brand. Through their backgrounds, they've used their experience to design the Airbnb business for trust so that all participating parties are satisfied and inspired by the business model with a great user experience (Greylock, 2015).

How Does Airbnb Work?

As already outlined in the founder story, you do not necessarily need to own any property to start in this business. If you have a spare bedroom or unit from where you already have a lease agreement, you can simply get permission from your landlord to sublet that space to guests who are either in your area for a specific event, or are there for a longer period but not long enough for them to take a leasing agreement. This could even be your own home if you are an empty nester.

What this business entails is registering a free account on the Airbnb website, describing yourself, and listing your property in a way that will attract guests. Describe your property in detail, paying attention to mention attractions around it, its unique selling point, and anything that makes it an ideal home that a guest would feel comfortable to live in. Because travelers are looking for comfort and a relaxing space, showcase your furnished property in such a manner that it draws in guests with a homey feel and privacy details, if that's the angle you're going for. Throw in local hangouts that are in the vicinity of your nest, amenities that come with the property, like free Wi-Fi, an emergency power bank, free parking, Jacuzzi, easy access to attractions, and emergency services so that guests feel secure.

Invest in a professional photographer that will showcase the beauty and warmth of your place and its ambience. After creating your detailed bio as a host and getting verified by Airbnb, you can start listing your property by giving it an attentive revamp, a great pitch that addresses your ideal guest, and an irresistible offer that makes it a go-to area or a must-have experience. Depending on what you're skilled at, what you enjoy doing, or what you feel like guests would be interested in, list your services in that manner to attract guests to book an experience.

Once you've listed your property, guests all over the world can see it on the Airbnb marketplace by searching your location or certain keywords that relate to your listing. Airbnb users can then book your property and pay through to the website, so that you don't have to deal with chancers yourself. As the host, you have the right to vet the guest to see whether you would be comfortable accommodating them. Similarly, guests also need to create their accounts and get verified in order to book listed properties.

THE POPULARITY OF AIRBNB

Why Is Airbnb So Popular?

▷ **Cost-Effective**

Contrary to hotels that need to meet certain criteria to be able to compete in upmarket areas, get their hospitality license, and offer standardized amenities, Airbnb has low start-up costs. Getting started is easy and cheap as you use the resources, space, or property that you already have. Because start-up costs and overhead expenses are kept at a minimum, you are able to offer competitive and irresistible offers to your guests.

Airbnb is thus cost-effective for both the host and the guest.

▷ Convenience

It can be intimidating to go into the hospitality industry as a beginner and complex without the required experience. For someone who wants to succeed in the hotel business, they would need more commitment as it requires a lot to set it up. Airbnb, on the other hand, is convenient as you don't need to disrupt your life or take any drastic measures to get started. You simply use what you have and enhance it. You don't need to uproot your life to make space for your guests if you're using the same property that you've listed on Airbnb. It's a convenient way to learn the details of the business from a close range, and only expand to other areas when you are financially and skillfully able to handle it.

For guests, Airbnb is convenient because one lives just like they would live in their own house where they can use appliances as they wish. Guests end up living like locals whereas at the hotel, a guest remains a guest with limited access to facilities that do not come with the room they paid for.

▷ Household Amenities

Most Airbnb guests are looking for fully-equipped houses with household amenities. This allows them to save on dinners by cooking their own meals and doing their own laundry which are prohibited or costly at hotels. Users of the Airbnb services already know that each home is different and thus offers different amenities. Guests know that your home is not a hotel, therefore they don't expect you to have separate appliances. What you already have as appliances can be shared with your guests without a need to buy a separate set. However, there are standard amenities that Airbnb requires, which we'll expand on further in the book.

▷ **Flexibility**

Guests love Airbnb because they can extend their stays, which means they can afford to stay longer in an area they love because they would have saved on accommodation and meals. If the schedule allows, check-in and check-out times are quite flexible at no extra cost in Airbnbs than in hotels. There's no need to follow standard protocol to speak to the manager; guests and hosts can flexibly shuffle things around.

The Types of Airbnb Customers

It is important to know the frequent users of Airbnb, as this indicates their preferences. Knowing what to offer your guests before they ask for it will make you a better host who is deemed to be attentive to detail. From your market research, which is more detailed in Chapter 3, you have to establish the kind of guests that visit your area, whether it's because of its incredible location, business, adventure, or any personal activities. That will then lead to knowing the possible reasons why they prefer Airbnb to hotels in your area. From the research conducted by Professor Daniel Guttentag, it was established that most Airbnb users were motivated by low costs, convenient location, household amenities, and flexibility (EHL Insights, n.d.).

▷ **Money Savers**

As previously mentioned, Airbnb prices are relatively lower than hotel prices and that is what motivates this group of users. People who want to save money, are on a low budget, or those who want to extend their stay usually look for cheaper accommodation. Money savers are usually young travelers who are explorative and looking for entertainment outside of the Airbnb itself. This means that, usually, they are there for things around your location and may want to save on accommodation and meals so as to fit in more activities or stay longer in your area. Money savers are usually not fussy about luxurious amenities, but they prefer that the essentials are provided. Giving them more than what they expect makes it highly likely that they will give you a great review, refer their friends and family, or return to your property in the future.

▷ Home Seekers

Home seekers are travelers who prefer a 'homey' feel than a structured hotel where one can constantly feel like a guest. This kind of guest prefers a "home away from home" vibe, a house fully-equipped with appliances. Accommodating home seekers means your home should have a stocked kitchen, larger living room, home appliances like a washer, dryer, and ironing board, amongst other things. Professor Guttentag's findings also revealed that home seekers tend to be older guests, group travelers, and frequent Airbnb users who usually stay longer. Home seekers can also be likened to pragmatic novelty seekers, who go for Airbnb for the household amenities, even though the latter are not as frequent users as home seekers.

▷ Collaborators

Collaborative consumers are usually drawn to Airbnb by the sharing economy philosophy. Unlike the above types who may prefer privacy and less interaction with the host, collaborators tend to prefer a local experience and love to explore hosts' recommendations. Another category that is very similar to collaborators is called interactive novelty seekers, who are also looking for authentic Airbnb experiences in a shared economy.

How to Attract a Specific Type of Guest

From the above categories, we can further narrow them down so that you know how to furnish your property to appeal to a certain group or groups. For instance, if you want to attract business travelers, your property needs to be in a quieter area with technological amenities like fast Wi-Fi, extra adapters, an espresso machine, and your pictures should also feature a working table. Including estimated distance and time to get around facilities they are likely to use, like the airport, the subway, or the convenience store will appear efficient as this type of guest often prefers to have easy access to their immediate needs. Business travelers may appreciate luxury toiletries or other personalized services like laundry and shopping offers at a good price.

Traveling couples are likely to prefer a more secluded location with privacy and a cozier feel. Preparing for them requires you to consider doubling some amenities to show that you were expecting a pair. Concentrate on listing romantic activities to do and restaurants around your area. You can feature a well-presented bed, flowers, bottle of wine, candles, a love seat, or anything that sparks romance. Attracting family guests may require you to child-proof your home—mention and show that your home is child-friendly with pictures of staircase gates, pool covers, and the closest parks with play areas.

Large groups of travelers will most likely prefer an entire home to themselves which offers more sleeping area and a spacious living room. Mentioning the large parking space, garage, or carports will appeal to them. You can also go the extra mile and source group discounts with local hangouts or adventurous activities. Another underrated and most considerate feature to mention is wheelchair ramp entrances or ease of access by persons with disabilities. Think ahead in order to design your property to attract your ideal client or not limit the diversity of guests you might accommodate in the future.

Why Is Airbnb So Unique?

▷ **It Focuses on the Customer Experience**

The goal of Airbnb is to offer users what they cannot get in hotels. It is structured to appeal to clients by making them the primary focus, providing to their needs, and making them feel taken care of. As much as hosts must take care of their property, they go out of their way to make the guest experience better. Unlike hotels that offer a standard treatment, Airbnb offers different options aimed to wow the guest. A guest can experience the thrill of living like a backpacker, be it in a boathouse, cabin, or a castle, depending on the experience that the host offers.

▷ It Keeps Things Intimate for the Traveler

With Airbnb, every guest is different, and the goal is to make it special for each at a time. Hotels are public places with a standard treatment whereas Airbnb keeps things intimate for each traveler, maintaining the original brand while reimagining and redefining the culture of creativity. Operations are not stereotypical or predictable like one would expect in hotels.

▷ It's Quite Fun

With hotels, the treatment is a professional one that cannot be deviated from, but with Airbnb, both the host and the guest can look forward to something exciting. Founders of Airbnb made friends from their guests and so do the hosts today. As much as they do things professionally, they open a room to get a little personal. For instance, even if the host does not meet the guests in person, they do leave recommendations of their favorite restaurants, activities, and authentic experiences that guests can look forward to. For hosts in a shared economy, they have an opportunity to make friends with people from all over the world, which is quite fun and flavorful. Guests get the opportunity to live in someone's house and live like a local at an affordable price. With endless possibilities and options like treehouses, houseboats, and even castles listed on Airbnb, that's an adventure waiting to happen (Whitmore, 2019).

THE PROS AND CONS OF AIRBNB

The Pros

✛ High Potential for Extra Income

One of the best reasons to venture into Airbnb is the high potential for earning an extra income through the space that could be idling. If you already own a property and are living on it, you can make an extra buck by simply sharing it on short-term rentals. This extra income can even help you to pay for the long-term mortgage, saving you from dipping into your personal savings. Depending on your occupancy rate, income from Airbnb can be really good, not only to help you cover the mortgage but to also have more money to reinvest in the business or use it to pursue the rest of your dreams.

✛ You Set Your Own Price

Every host is different, so is every home. There is no preset pricing rule which allows hosts the flexibility to collect the money that they want for their property. This means that you can do a promotion for your guests or special discounts as you wish. Moreover, you can adjust the price as you see fit during peak season. Depending on the uniqueness of your listing, you can make tons of money through Airbnb.

✛ Variety of Listings

Airbnb is the reason people are now able to rent cabins in exotic places, treehouses, houseboats, and even castles. There's a wide selection of properties you can list on Airbnb. Guests get to experience their wildest dreams without the commitment of owning exotic properties. Hosts get to think out of the box to keep feeding the hungry market with spectacular listings. This allows the owners to remodel and repurpose any item that they thought was obsolete. Because Airbnb's unique selling point is experience, hosts are faced with various options to make their guests have a memorable experience, whether it's at the lake house, caravan, tiny home, container house, or igloo. The possibilities are endless and exciting for both the hosts and the guests.

✚ Airbnb Has Helpful Resources for Hosts

As opposed to starting a hospitality business on your own with no support, getting started on Airbnb is a great way to learn the business with the free resources that are at the disposal of every registered user. There are numerous helpful resources and tips on how to succeed in this business. You can reach out to the resource center and have any issues you might have resolved. There are tips for anything regarding managing your Airbnb, scaling your Airbnb, things you need to achieve and maintain superhost status, and a forum dedicated to helping you become a successful host.

✚ Protection for Both Host and Guest

The major obstacle or objection angle that the founders of Airbnb quickly sought to curb—even before it brought problems—is safety for the key players in this business model. As already mentioned, the founders designed Airbnb for trust in order to protect everyone. Guests might have been hesitant to pay for a stranger's home instead of a reputable hotel, simply because of fear that the owner might do a runner or turn out to be a disappointment as people could lie on their profiles. Airbnb holds the guest's payment for 24 hours after check-in before releasing it to the host so that should the guest feel like they are not satisfied with the property—say, because it's dirty or the host lied about some amenities in their listing—Airbnb refunds the guest their money.

On the other hand, hosts that feared that their property might be trashed by guests can claim from Airbnb which covers hosts up to $1 million for damaged property. The guest is also asked to pay for damaged property, and since they have to be identity verified prior to making a booking, they are traceable and they can be banned from ever using the service again. This protection binds every party to act on good will by either becoming a responsible guest who respects other people's property or by becoming a trustworthy host who goes out of their way to make the guest feel welcome.

✚ You Can Manage Everything on Your Own

Even with no prior experience, finding your feet is not as hard as establishing other businesses that require specialized skills. As a homeowner, you already know how to run a home. Managing an Airbnb business is just an intentional effort to be more accommodating, make people feel welcomed, and have patience with others. As a beginner, you can take on a load that you can handle until you've made enough profits to automate the system so that it operates smoothly, even without your active involvement.

✚ Free Listing

The major upside for the hosts is to be able to freely list their property to the existing millions of Airbnb users across the world. To have your property listed on your local media house or on popular online marketplaces requires you to allocate specific funds, whereas with Airbnb, your property gets exposed to numerous people who already use the service. You can showcase photos of your property with great descriptions or catchy captions, and your user profile presents you as an ideal host for free. With the use of the right keywords, not only will your listed property be exposed to active users of the Airbnb platform, but it may also find its way to rise to the top search of the search engines, where even non-Airbnb users will see it and get on the platform just to access your property.

The Cons

— Hosting Takes a Lot of Work

Prior to the actual work of getting the business off the ground, let me tell you that the first real work you have to do is on you. As you are starting out, you may be looking at people who make it look so easy—because it really is once you crack the code—and raise your expectations that it will be like that for you. Bear in mind that you will be dealing with different people on a daily basis. This means that today you can accommodate a considerate guest who cleans after themselves and treats your property with respect. The next guest can be a complete opposite who tests your last nerve, and you have to treat both with the same amicable attitude and be more tolerant so you don't sweat the small stuff.

Hosting takes a lot of work, marketing, customer relations and interpersonal skills, patience, emotional toll, and physical strength to be able to handle the responsibility that comes with it. It takes serious effort to be able to accommodate people with different personalities and characters into your personal space. Before you get to expand into properties that are designed to accommodate guests, you would have had to deal with a lot of turmoil to plant your feet firmly in this business. In the beginning, before you earn profits, you will need more time to ensure that your business runs smoothly, your property maintains a level of neatness, and you go beyond your call of duty to make your guests feel more at home. Even to achieve the Superhost status is something that will require you to put in the effort into the business and throw in your special touch in order to attract those positive reviews (No-Nonsense Airbnb, 2021).

Although it's not always the financial requirements—having a strong financial boost goes a long way in setting your standard as early as possible—hosting takes a lot from you. Nonetheless, the benefits usually offset the cons. Moreover, as you make money, you can reinvest it by integrating a property management service (PMS) which will save you a ton of time and money through automation and improve your business efficiency (Robuilt, 2022).

▬ There Are Unpredictable Situations

Like with any business, there are risks involved in the Airbnb business. There are usually unforeseen circumstances that are unavoidable. Since you would've opened your home to many people, you might find that your property wears down quicker. From dealing with clogged toilets, broken appliances, or disgruntled guests, being an Airbnb host can be stressful—not only entailing possible damage to your property, but with the guests' well-being, as well. Anything that happens to a guest while they are in your property is a liability to you and the future of your business. Just as with Uber or Lyft transport services, some hotels and Airbnbs have been used for suicide, human trafficking, substance abuse, and different kinds of assault launch pads (Lieber, 2015).

These are possibilities that can happen even in your property. I'm not trying to scare you off the business, but it's best that you know so that you put the necessary security measures and insurance in place for such unpredictable situations. The founders of Airbnb are aware of these minorities, and while some are hard to avoid before they happen, the percentage of these incidents is relatively small. It's wise to be aware should anything peculiar happen in your property. Airbnb provides a limited cover of up to $1 million towards damaged property, even though not everything can be replaced.

— Legal Implications

If not handled properly, Airbnb business could be illegal. It's paramount that you understand what legal implications, land restrictions, tax laws, and lease agreements apply in your area before you start on the wrong foot. Some places and types of properties require a special permit prior to operating an Airbnb. Some state laws require that hosts don't rent out spaces that they are not living in a certain number of days per year, which means that if not carefully done, one may rush to scale and use properties that they are not using as their residence, thereby breaking the law and being faced with atrocious consequences (9NEWS, 2019). It is thus important to conduct a thorough research on zoning ordinances so as to know what is allowed or prohibited.

— Longer Booking Process

This is a pain for guests who prefer less interaction online, as they would normally select a room at a hotel's website and make a payment instantly. As a precautionary measure, some hosts want to be able to vet the guest before they allow them to book their place. This means that the guest needs to create an account with Airbnb, verify their identity, and also work on getting reviews. In that process, the guest might lose their patience and decide to go with another host or a different booking platform. Airbnb guests need an identity-verified profile and good reviews to be credible. Hosts may be skeptical to accept guests with no reviews and whose identity has not been verified by Airbnb. Overall, this can be a lengthier process for both the guest and the host.

THE HOSTS OF AIRBNB

What Are Hosts?

An Airbnb host is someone who is primarily listed on the Airbnb marketplace in the property listing. Regardless of who manages the property, handles the communication, or who ensures that the property is bringing in revenue, Airbnb allows one primary host who appears on the platform. A host can be the property owner, manager, or anyone who guests will find when they arrive at the property, if it's not self check-in. There are types of hosts who play different roles in the hosting business. Airbnb requires that hosts do the following duties.

▷ Be Responsive

Hosts are required to keep their response rate high by replying to trip bookings and inquiries in under 24 hours in order to avoid making guests wait. The host whose response rate is low loses money, as guests always prefer to have their queries attended to as timely as possible. The hosts who keep a high response rate also boost their search algorithm so they show up high in the search results.

▷ Accept Trip Requests

Accepting trip requests is one of the important roles of hosts, unless they have set an instant booking feature with which Airbnb can accept bookings from guests instantly, provided the calendar shows availability of the property.

▷ Welcome Guests

Airbnb requires that hosts are there to welcome guests into their property. This does not have to be in person, but there should be no communication breakdown between the host and the guest from the time of booking to the arrival and welcoming of guests into the property.

▷ Get and Give Reviews

Reviews help both the guest and the host as they determine their next booking. Guests that have received negative reviews of trashing the host's property or were reported to be rude might struggle to get their bookings accepted elsewhere. Hosts exist to offer a service, and this service can be reviewed if it meets the standards of Airbnb. For instance, a host must not cancel guest bookings unless there are inescapable circumstances, and they will have to prove to Airbnb that such an incident occured. Any negative reviews that the host gets hurt their chances of being booked. The role of the host is thus to deliver exceptional service so as to attract great reviews. Hosts also need to give reviews to their guests so as to also increase their review ratings. Giving reviews also sets the standard, as the guests who read reviews by hosts know how their actions make them feel and are likely to be more considerate.

The Types of Hosts

▷ The Listing Owner

The listing owner is someone who opens the account on Airbnb marketplace as the primary host. This is someone who has all the admin access to appoint any co-hosts or manage the account themselves. It could be the property owner or manager who can prove to Airbnb that they have permission to lease their property to guests. The listing owner is also a primary host or one that ensures that the operations are running smoothly. They have permissions to accept bookings, appoint co-hosts, edit the calendar, process payments, access the transaction history, and list or delist the property. Their primary job is to ensure that their Airbnb business is profitable, whether it's through personally handling things or through automation so that they spend more time looking for more properties to list.

▷ The Co-Host

The role of the co-host is to relieve listing owners from some duties for a management fee. Airbnb describes a co-host as someone who could be a friend or family member who covers for the primary hosts when they are unavailable. They have limited permissions but can do the most to ensure that bookings are done, guests are responded to on time, the property is stocked with supplies, ensure that check-in and checkout are smooth, and the cleaning team has been contacted. A co-host has permission to create and edit a property listing, add titles, descriptions, photos, update calendar, and determine pricing. They can also accept or reject reservations, message guests, ensure that the property is guest-ready, and even welcome guests in person. Moreover, co-hosts can write reviews, contact the resolution center, and get support from Airbnb.

▷ **The Hosting Team**

The hosting team, which may comprise a company or group of people, manages the short-term or long-term rentals on behalf of the owner or the renter. The hosting team is required when you have multiple properties or when you prefer to be hands-off for the business. Similar to co-hosts, the hosting team has permissions to run and do numerous tasks for the owner. The person who sets up this team owns the main account, then appoints co-hosts to manage listings, manage the property, accept or decline reservations, handle payments, and contact support when needed. The hosting team breaks down all the tasks for managing an Airbnb smoothly. The hosting team consists of the account owner, task and finance teams, guest management, listing management, and team management.

The account owner has no restrictions regarding what they are permitted to do. They can appoint every team member and even contact the resolution center addressing any situation faced by the member of the team. The tasks team can view their assigned tasks, update their progress, and verify completion once they are done, as well as report if there are any breakages. This team includes cleaners and maintenance workers. Task members are limited to these permissions only. Another group that has bigger responsibilities is the listing team. The listing team can create new property listings, snooze, delist, or resume listings, set pricing—discounts, fees, smart pricing, currency settings, and nightly price—and update tax details for each listing. This team can also manage reservations, create tasks, and assign tasks. The guest management team has permissions to accept or decline reservations, write and respond to guest reviews, handle all guest requirements and communication, as well as permission to assign tasks. The finance team has access to the transaction history, can review reservation earnings, and can generate earnings and payout reports.

KEY POINTS

- Airbnb started from humble beginnings—and so can you. Depending on your dedication and effort, it is easy to grow from one spare room to having a multi-home or several properties anywhere in the world.
- For a business that started over a decade ago, Airbnb is still in its infancy stage with a plethora of opportunities for beginners, experienced realtors, and people who want to make their mark in the hospitality industry.
- Considering the different reasons why people travel and seek accommodation, this is not a market that can be easily exhausted, meaning it's not too late for you to begin today. Also, getting started on the Airbnb platform is not as hard as you think.
- You can design for a successful Airbnb business if you know your type of guest, their reason to visit your area, how you can attract them, and how to wow them with a service that will leave them no choice but give you great reviews.
- As long as you offer irresistible offers on your property that beat the hotel stay, there is no limit to what you can achieve in this industry.

Now that the mystery behind Airbnb has been solved and you now have basic knowledge of this business model, the next chapter will give you the details of investing in Airbnb. You will also determine if the business is worth it from the host and investor perspective.

2

INVESTING IN AIRBNB—IS IT WORTH THE EFFORT?

When COVID-19 hit and international travel was banned, related businesses took the biggest hit. Travel bloggers and content creators Siya and Kristen, like anyone whose income was affected, were frustrated by the subsequent lockdowns, wondering how they would afford their free-spirited lifestyle. On top of their financial woes, this travel couple had just taken out a mortgage on a mountain paradise with one of the most to die for scenic views. Just as with the classic Airbnb founders' tale, Siya and Kristen discovered that they could rent out their beautiful new crib to local travelers and give them an exquisite experience in their home. They cleaned their home, set out to have great photos for it, signed up for a free account on the Airbnb platform, and they listed their property.

To this couple's astonishment, their listing had already been hit with 13 requests within a day, during the pandemic, when hotels and flights were closing shop. In one month, their crib on Airbnb had brought in over $10,000, which not only covered the mortgage, renovations, bills, and their lifestyle of luxury, but also unlocked the potential of Airbnb to change the couple's mindset: finding this unique setting of Airbnb and hosting people who want a genuine experience while living in someone's house without a need to travel somewhere fancy and abroad. These lovebirds knew that their worries were a thing of the past when the Airbnb listing was able to cover their expenses and maintain their lifestyle, even though they were fairly new into the industry, amazed by the endless possibilities that this business model offers (Sarah, 2021).

THE AIRBNB INVESTMENT

The Statistics

As of 2021 end of year statistics, Airbnb amassed a total revenue of over $5.9 billion, over 300 million bookings, and over 150 million users. There are over 6 million listings around the world in at least 100,000 cities and 220 countries (Curry, 2020). Despite the global pandemic—which took even some giant hotels out of business—the hospitality industry continues to grow and people continue to travel the world. Users of Airbnb continue to grow amidst the pandemic, with an influx of cabin bookings and experiences between 2020 and 2022. For a platform that has over 15 years of service, it's easy to think that it has run its course, considering the growing competition. You might even think that you're late or wonder if it's worth the effort. We'll discuss how to handle Airbnb as an investment, crunch the numbers, and come up with the answer to the question: Why should you invest?

▷ A Great Track Record

So far, Airbnb's track record of success is mind-blowing. The exponential growth of this company, as evidenced by the success stories of ordinary people from across the world, shows that it is headed in the right direction. While it faces a healthy competition with other start-ups in the short-term rental niche, Airbnb has proven that it's here to stay. Besides actively taking part in the Airbnb business, it's also lucrative to invest in Airbnb as a listed company with a healthy growth circle. While it's an older company, it only has less than five years as a publicly listed company, providing a greater room for growth as travel restrictions are lifted after the worst times of the global pandemic (Santoro, 2022).

▷ **Intercultural Diversity**

Most experiences offered on Airbnb are authentic local experiences and activities that introduce guests to intercultural diversities, which in turn improve humanity as we tend to understand and embrace our differences. Taking part in this model is opening up to this diversity.

▷ **Long-Term Rental Option**

Airbnb is becoming more common for long-term stays, which means it has marked its territory beyond the hospitality business and is expanding into real estate. While short-term rentals are usually more profitable, there's stability in long-term rentals, and Airbnb has gravitated towards this model. There's a shift in travel as longer bookings increase the occupancy rate and, thus, the company as a whole makes more money.

▷ **Airbnb's Platform Continues to Evolve**

After CEO Brian Chesky took to Twitter and asked the community to suggest upgrades for the Airbnb platform, over 150 upgrades have already been rolled out in the first quarter of 2022, with more to be considered from the 4,000 responses to Chesky's post (Santoro, 2022). The current upgrades show a great improvement in the user interface and experience for both the hosts and guests. For a company that wants to improve its conduct and involve the users in its upgrades, investors can find this positive as it shows potential of growth when the upgrades are integrated and new users are attracted to the platform.

▷ Potential to Earn High Profits

Looking at the stock price of Airbnb, there is a high potential to make profits as the price has corrected around $120–$130 per share, which leaves room to grow towards and beyond its all time high of $220 per share. In other words, this price drop has allowed investors to get into this trade and acquire more stock for this evolutionary company.

Is It a Safe Investment?

The Pros

✚ It's Safer Than Lucrative Traditional Renting

A monthly rent is relatively lower than a nightly charge for the same unit. For example, a unit that costs about $2,000 a month can bring in $180 per night. With an occupancy rate of at least 67%—meaning if it's occupied for only 20 days, of which some Airbnbs have even a higher occupancy rate—the same unit can bring in about $3,600 minus the service and cleaning fees. This is in relation to the safety of an investment; in the event that a guest or tenant moves out of a long-term rental unit, it can take a while for the vacant property to be filled, therefore causing the owner to lose a whole month's rent. With Airbnb, even if not all days are occupied, the income from the nights that the property was booked is enough to cover costs and leave the host with good profits (Lemke, 2022).

✚ You Will Have a Diverse Portfolio of Clients

As opposed to putting your eggs in one basket with one tenant, you can have different guests on a daily, weekly, or monthly basis on Airbnb. This means that your portfolio is more diversified with short-term occupants than one long-term tenant. If the tenant is great and pays the rent on time, a traditional rental business might be safer. But if the client leaves without paying, your expected rent can be negatively affected, and this might also cause a disruption while you wait to get another tenant. But with Airbnb, even if one guest cancels their booking, you still have more days to allow others to book so that you can quickly curb the effects of that potential loss of income. Additionally, cancellation doesn't mean you have to give a full refund, meaning you can still make money.

The Cons

— It Can Be Risky to Your Wallet

Harboring a long-term tenant could be cheaper than having to impress multiple different Airbnb guests. You need to have a steady cash flow if you have daily or weekly guests with different preferences coming to your property. As you strive to be a great host, you may find yourself spending more every now and then, trying to accommodate and make a good impression on your guests. But with a tenant, the only expenses can just be utilities, maintenance once in a while, or mowing the lawn. Some tenants take care of these things in exchange for cheaper rent.

— Possible Instability of Income

Airbnb income is irregular as it is dependent on peak or off-seasons. This is not the case with the rental business as the agreed amount of rent will be paid monthly regardless of the season. Some months when there is an influx of bookings at a normal or higher rate, you may have to save that money to carry you through during the dry season. Unlike long-term rentals where you know that for the duration of the lease you're guaranteed to collect rent, this is not the case with Airbnb as scheduled bookings can change abruptly.

— Even With Success, It Can Still Be Slow Growth

The success of Airbnb is usually dependent on your credibility as a host, which may be difficult when you're starting out because you may not have enough reviews. Airbnb success is gradual, and as specified above, irregular income may be difficult to predict the future success of your business.

A GOOD AIRBNB ROI

Before you spend your money on Airbnb, it is paramount that you familiarize yourself with some important aspects of the business. As much as it may sound exciting to host and bask in the fascinating experience, you need to think like a business person and crunch the numbers to see if it's viable for you. Below are some of the most noteworthy Airbnb metrics to consider.

Occupancy Rate

In layman's terms, the occupancy rate is the measure of how likely your Airbnb is to be booked. This ratio is derived by calculating the number of nights your Airbnb property is booked over the total number of nights it was listed or made available for booking throughout the year. This means that out of the nights that your property was made available for reservations, the number of nights that the property was occupied and paid for determines the occupancy rate. This metric is important as it determines the popularity of your establishment and, subsequently, its profitability. Depending on the location, season, level of service, and reviews, any occupancy rate that is 65% and above is deemed as profitable. Anything below 65% is an indication that your property is underperforming and you need to get to the bottom of the cause (Karani, 2020).

Once you've analyzed the real cause of your low occupancy rate, then you will be able to know which areas need more of your focus. Some areas like location and season may be out of your control, but your standard of hospitality and reviews are things that you can work on improving to see if there's any change in the occupancy rate. It's worth noting that you cannot pre-calculate this ratio before your establishment is on the market, but knowing how it's derived before embarking in the actual business will help you strive to fill your property with confirmed reservations when your business is operational.

It will also help you be more vigilant of the location of your property during the business plan stage, perform thorough market research to determine how properties in your area are performing, and work on delivering excellent service in order to secure great reviews. The higher your occupancy rate will be, the more profitable your property will be, and that is a good return on investment. The occupancy rate will determine the rate of return on your property investment, and it will affect other metrics like Airbnb rental income, cash flow, cap rate, and the overall ROI.

Airbnb Rental Income

Another important measure of your return on investment is Airbnb rental income, which is the amount of revenue that your property will bring on a periodic basis. As already mentioned, Airbnb rental income is reliant on the occupancy rate. It is also affected by other metrics like nightly rate, seasonality, and the location of the property. A rental property that is booked on a long-term period increases the chances of a higher rental income because the occupancy rate will also be high. The higher the rental income, the higher the rate of return on your property.

Airbnb Cash Flow

As with any business, the more cash flowing in and out of the business, the easier it is to run that business. In other niches, cash flow may be likened to liquidity of a business, with high liquidity being more preferred. Technically speaking, Airbnb cash flow determines the difference between the total rental income and the total rental expenses. This crucial metric is a great indication of the performance of your investment, with the rental income aimed to be higher than the expenses for a profit. The more positive your cash flow, the better the performance of your property; the more negative cash flow, which means expenses surpass income, the poorer your property is performing.

Airbnb ROI

Even more important than cash flow, Airbnb ROI is the most crucial metric to determine whether your Airbnb rental is profitable or not, whether you can afford to keep it up and running or whether it's digging up a deeper grave of debt for you. This tool that is used by most savvy investors prior to acquiring an Airbnb on sale is calculated as a measure of profitability of a property against its costs. ROI is expressed as a percentage, with anything ranging from 8–12% considered good ROI. While it's great to go for a property that shows potential for a higher ROI, sometimes it's considered a high risk.

ROI can be calculated in two ways: Airbnb *cap rate* and *cash on cash return*. The cap rate is the percentage of the net operating income (NOI) against its fair market value. NOI is determined by the difference between the annual rental income and the annual rental operating expenses. It differs from cash flow by excluding the cost of financing the property.

THINGS TO CONSIDER

Consideration #1: There Will Be Costs

▷ **Costs to Rent**

One of the most obvious costs of starting an Airbnb rental business is rent of the property. You need to consider the rental payment of the property you're leasing. Knowing this information beforehand is important and will play a bigger role in the nightly rate pricing of your property. You want the property that will generate money through a high occupancy rate so you will always have your rent covered. It's also important to note that regardless of whether your property is booked or not, you still have to pay a rental fee for it. This means you may need to have your rental fee upfront so that even if the money you make from bookings is delayed or inconsistent during a dry season, you don't lose your property or get in trouble with the landlord. Rental cost is one of the expenses that took out most hotels when the global pandemic hit. You also have to consider catering for rent even during circumstances that may affect your cash flow.

▷ Renovations

Whether you are using your own house or renting out space as your Aribnb, you need to consider that it may need serious renovations prior to its operation. Even a property that is already functional may need a touch up of renovations every now and then to either remain competitive with modern and lux hotels in the area or to maintain what might have broken during guest stays.

▷ Mortgages

If your Airbnb needs financing, one of the startup costs that you'll be faced with when you commence this business is the mortgage repayments. Irrespective of whether you're already realizing profits or not, the Airbnb mortgage needs to be considered as a recurring expense.

▷ Operating Costs

There are several running costs that you must consider as part of your periodical expenses of an Airbnb. Cleaning fees, supplies, or some amenities that need restocking after every guest checks out are considered as costs of operating the business. Sometimes, before your rental brings in enough revenue, it requires more from you to finance its costs of operation. Operating costs are like the overheads in hotels; whether the business is profitable or not, these costs must be catered for in order for the business to keep its doors open.

▷ Utility Costs

Without a doubt, your rental unit will consume electricity, water, and Wi-Fi, amongst other utilities. Things like smart locks need to be subscribed monthly, although they can either fall under bills or operating costs. As with the operating costs, utility bills need to be paid whether you've realized the profits or not, whether your rental maintained a high or low occupancy rate. These costs need to be considered and foreplanned so that your business doesn't run into more debt at its onset.

▷ Insurance

As mentioned before, Airbnb provides cover for up to $1 million for damaged property of Airbnb hosts. However, it's advisable to pay for your own additional insurance with a third party, as the one provided by Airbnb is limited or may be subject to terms and conditions. The last thing you want is going from pillar to post when you claim and your property is not bringing any income while you deal with a crisis. Should you take any insurance cover for your property, it will add to monthly costs that need to be considered.

Consideration #2: The Market Is Crowded

The hospitality business and real estate markets are where the masses are. The most wealthy have paved the way by doing property investments. The likes of Robert Kiyosaki and Grant Cardone have built massive wealth through real estate. Not only have the tycoons built for themselves, but they've brought along their mentees. The Airbnb business model was not new to begin with, as there already existed Vacation Rentals By Owners (VRBO) and HomeAway, among other platforms. Over the years, the market has grown exponentially, moreso because Airbnb has made entry into the industry super easy. It is important to note that this is a highly competitive market. Below are a few pointers to use when analyzing the Airbnb market.

▷ **Step 1: Find the Right Location**

You need to ask yourself questions regarding the location you're considering for your Airbnb. Is it in a prime location? What makes it ideal for your proposed business? What is the neighborhood like? Are there lots of things to do in that area? How far from the attractions will your Airbnb be? Your choice of location plays a vital role in determining how your Airbnb will perform seasonally.

▷ Step 2: Understand the Rules in Your Location

It is important to consider the regulations that apply in your area. Long-term and short-term rental rules differ from one state to another and one zone may allow a certain establishment while another zone restricts it.

▷ Step 3: Define Your Target Market

When pondering on the possible success of your Airbnb, you must have a picture of your ideal guests. What is your target market? Does it consist of solo travelers looking for an authentic local experience on a budget? Could it be business travelers looking for more technology-based amenities? You can define your own target market, analyze the kind of traveler they are, and build with that picture in mind, knowing how you will appeal to them.

▷ Step 4: Conduct a Competitor Analysis

What makes you think of starting your Airbnb business in your desired area? What have you identified as a gap to fill? What similar businesses exist in that area? What's your competitive edge? Do a thorough competitor analysis, pay attention to the pain points expressed by those who use competitive services, and aim at addressing their needs. Search for your direct competitors, the marketplaces they are listing on, their pricing plans, and study the reviews they get. Knowing your competition will give you an upper hand to build something unique and give you a competitive edge.

▷ **Step 5: Choose Your Tools for Market Analysis**

- **AirDNA**

AirDNA is one of the greatest data analyzing tools to deploy in order to run a successful operation. It extracts data from platforms such as Airbnb and VRBO, uses algorithms to match any properties that are listed on multiple platforms, syncs that data based on reservations, and finally updates that information on MarketMinder and Enterprise Data. AirDNA collects its data from individual hosts, property management services, channel managers, and scraped data from Airbnb and VRBO. Using advanced artificial intelligence and machine learning, AirDNA is able to determine the exact dates that properties were booked against days that the owners blocked their calendars for maintenance in order to retrieve accurate revenue reports for better market and profitability analysis. You can use AirDNA to determine the potential revenue that you can make from Airbnb in your desired location even before you make a commitment of buying or renting that property. As a beginner, you can use a free version of AirDNA that shows limited data, but when you want more accuracy and unlimited data tools, a paid version for your specific town will come in handy (Iacob, 2019).

- **Mashvisor**

Another incredible tool that you can use to analyze the Airbnb market in your intended location is Mashvisor. Mashvisor works similarly to AirDNA in that it gives you collected data from different channels that you can use to analyze the market and potential performance of your Airbnb prior to committing your efforts and funds. You need to know the location where you want to host your Airbnb, common events in the area, occupancy rate, nightly rate, and types of properties that resemble the one that you have in mind. Mashvisor collects this data and you can use this platform to customize your search to fit the exact similar property and see its performance in real time, which you will then use to decide if the area is ideal or if you need to browse further (Mashvisor, 2022).

- **Hosting Groups**

The hosting business has fairly run its course, and in the process produced a set of experienced individuals who are willing to share their knowledge with those who are new to the market for free. Facebook groups and online forums are great destinations to find free advice. Look for hosting groups in your specific area of interest and start learning what has been shared already. You can also throw in your question to get responses from people who can prove that they have real world experience before you use the analytical tools above, or you can leverage all of them for a deeper search (Griffiths, 2020).

Consideration #3: The Airbnb Team

How do you plan on handling the business? Will you be fully hands-on, hosting with a partner, or will you completely leave it in the hands of a professional? Ask yourself if you need to hire a real estate agent, and if you do, find out where you will find one who qualifies for what you have in mind. Going with a real estate agent can save you a lot of trouble choosing property in a location that might not be optimal. There are things that these agents are accustomed to that may not be easily accessible information to someone who is not in their circle. If you want to save time and money, you may need to search online, check print ads, or ask around for the best realtors from other professionals, and vet them.

Now that you know how to find the best real estate agent, the next step is to determine your Airbnb team based on how you plan to run the business. It's possible to own a property that fits the Airbnb business model. But you may not want to be hands-on with the hospitality and interacting with guests. Maybe you may have other responsibilities and no time to run this business. Narrow down your options and analyze what you need to know before you hire a property manager or assign co-hosts.

Consideration #4: Success Is Gradual

You need to bear in mind that things won't happen as quickly as you may like them to and build with patience. With determination, you can achieve your goals as long as you are realistic. Take time to assess your business plan; scrutinize your idea and find a firm reason that will serve as a pulling or pushing effect on days that you feel like you're not cut out for this. Success does not happen overnight, and even the people who inspire you built gradual wealth. Getting closer to them might reveal the hidden struggle stories and sacrifices they endured before they reached their public glories. Consider that it may take time before you record great success in this business, and make peace with it so that you can give yourself grace for your efforts, applauding that each day you're a step further than you were a day before.

KEY POINTS

- Considering the growing numbers pertaining to the Airbnb business model from either an investor's perspective or getting first-hand experience at hosting, Airbnb is not something you take with a grain of salt. It might be the most lucrative opportunity you stumble on.
- As with any great business start-up, it is wise to crunch the numbers, get knowledge on the important figures that will determine your revenue, and understand the possible return on investment your decision will bring.
- Use the available tools like AirDNA or Mashvisor to analyze the market and potential of your intended establishment. Get even more personal by joining hosting groups to get personal experience and advice from real people.

- Understand that there will be costs every step of the way, you won't realize profits right away, and success is a long game.
- You also need to bear in mind that you are entering an already populated niche, so it's wise that you understand your competitive edge and what you need to do to up your game.

In the next chapter, you will learn the first step in starting your Airbnb journey: analyzing the market around you in order to determine your plan of action to ride this wave of wealth with the intention to succeed.

3

THE BASE OF YOUR AIRBNB BUSINESS

For a business that started 15 years ago, Airbnb is currently valued at over $93.01 billion, about 8.4% down since the start of 2022. It's all-time high valuation in 2021 was $110 billion. While this benchmark is a wildest dream for the founders, considering how they incubated this idea with mishaps during its start-up, this business model has not only enriched the founders but has and continues to change lives of many people around the globe. The average host earns around $13,800 annually, with superhosts making way more than this figure. Interestingly, over 1 billion bookings have been recorded on Airbnb, indicating the massiveness of this business, which might make you wonder what the future holds for this business (Jaleesa, 2018).

In this chapter, we will tackle the basics of starting the Airbnb business, from generating a comprehensive business plan to understanding the rules and regulations governing this business model. Knowing this information will help you to start your business with the right tools that will act as a firm foundation for profitable and legal establishment.

THE BUSINESS PLAN

With the statistics shared in our opening paragraph, it shows that you can achieve tremendous results with your Airbnb business if you set your mind to it. The key to success is to have a detailed business plan that will outline your roadmap. Another thing is that your business plan will structure your journey, vividly indicate where you need to put more focus, motivate you as you tick things off your to-do list, and act as a compass to navigate your way in this business.

Creating the Business Plan

▷ Step #1: Create Your Mission Statement

What are your goals with this business? Are you looking to solve temporary cash flow, or do you have a dream of making this your core business? One of the greatest keys to a functional mission statement is being honest with yourself. Remember that this is your business, so it has to be ideal for you, serve you first, and not only make you lots of money, but it must bring you joy and fulfillment. You want to set goals that are more personal so that even when things get a bit tricky, your long-term goal is bigger than a temporary setback.

If this is a temporary solution to your cash flow problems and not something you actually love, be prepared that while you will make money, it will be a daunting task that might take its toll on you. So, think vigorously about your goals with this business. Be honest with what you want to achieve from venturing into Airbnb and then create your mission statement from it. Your mission statement will act as a reminder of why you started and why you still hold on amidst foreseeable challenges.

If your goal is to belong to a certain financial bracket, then you will know how much effort you should input in order to reach that level. If you have a dream to be one of the most successful property or hospitality moguls in your area, you will work towards attaining that level at all costs. If your dream is to spend more time with your loved ones, travel the world, help others, and give your family the best version of the life you have envisioned, it will take work and determination to build a firmly founded business that follows core principles, maintains your set standards, and becomes the fulfillment of your wildest dreams.

Another core principle that will help you craft a functional mission statement is surrounding yourself with your inspiration. What inspires you to want a successful outcome in this business? Do you see the inspiring life of Grant Cardone, the exponential growth of Cardone Capital, and feel motivated? Do you see the Marriott, Hilton, and other noteworthy hospitality-based businesses thriving and wonder what it takes to reach that level? Regardless of how wild your dream is, if you constantly feed on the kind of inspirational content that ignites your fire, there is no limit to how far you can go. So, as you draft your mission statement, take time to study your inspiration and you will be able to have a mission that seems bigger than you at first until you actually accomplish it.

In the hospitality business, it doesn't matter much the amount of money you make if your service is poor. We've seen well-known companies with state of the art facilities losing their crowns to secondary companies because of bad reviews (Rhodes, 2019). You want to offer the best hospitality you can, and this mission statement has to be visible to all your staff and any third parties you may choose to partner with. A great service goes a long way in this industry. Yes, guests appreciate great amenities and irresistible prices, but they appreciate the experience of being in your property more. Let the lasting memory they have of your place be a pleasant and warm one.

The values that you want to uphold are what your guests will rave about. You want them to feel welcomed and appreciated. The reasons why people may choose your Airbnb differ. One may be looking at accommodation for travel purposes, whereas one may just want a different experience from their own homes. We have people planning romantic getaways in fancy hotels in their vicinity just to feel pampered, while others book Airbnb listed cabins or exotic treehouses for the edgy encounter. Regardless of the location, hospitality has everything to do with great values. In your mission statement, you want these values stipulated so that your team knows you have a standard to maintain.

You want a level of immaculate neatness maintained from reception to guestrooms, and as far as the bathroom—especially the bathroom! You want efficiency of the tools you use to be something to speak about. Your response to your guests need to be on par if you want to be amongst the best performing hosts. The value that your guests get from you, whether it is politeness or excellent service, is what will make you last long in this industry. Therefore, you have to be intentional with what you want to be known for. A bold mission statement is the lifeblood of your business plan and a driving force towards a successful business; that is the reason every successful business has one.

▷ **Step #2: Include Your Marketing Analysis**

A great business plan includes proper market research about your niche and sub-niches. You need to know all the demographics surrounding your business. Where are you located or where do you want your business to be based? Who is your competition? What is the average occupancy rate and turnover that similar businesses are making? You want to know these metrics before you start with your business so that you have a benchmark and a plan to perform above average. Find out where your competition is coming short and design your business to solve those problems so that you set yourself apart from the rest. Find the pain points of guests that use facilities near you or anywhere you want to position your Airbnb, then aim at becoming the solution.

What kind of amenities do you want to offer? What does your competition offer? As part of your market research, some of these questions will not be answered from external surveys only. You will need to book into your competitors for that first-hand experience. What did you like about what their rooms offer? What did you wish was provided but was not? Answering these questions will help you set up the amenities for your property. Of course, you need to meet Airbnb's basic requirements before you think of revamping what others are offering. Your personal touch goes a long way to make guests feel welcomed and considered in your business. Include them in your business plan so that they are well accounted for when you do your financial plan.

Conducting market research will also help you with your pricing plan. Knowing what your competition charges based on their service will help in designing your own pricing plan. You don't really need to make your place cheap in order to beat the competition. Some people just want great hospitality and they are prepared to pay any amount of money to get it. So, don't be afraid to plan the standard you want to maintain in your Airbnb; that will help you to come up with a realistic price plan. Remember that you are running a business which must yield profits for you. Your business plan has to include what you aim to do differently from your competition. What will be your unique selling point?

The great thing about marketing research when it comes to financial planning is that you can design to have irresistible offers. Great offers are not always cheap, but anything that a client feels like they have ripped you off is near perfect. Of course, they would not have bankrupted you because the reason you do this ahead is so that you can find ways to minimize the costs of your excellent service. Whether you have to negotiate better deals with suppliers or have to source alternatives at a steal, your advantage is knowing these things beforehand, prior to the operation of your business. This leads to the next step of your business plan.

▷ **Step #3: Consider Your Budget**

Generally speaking, starting an Airbnb business would not require you to rob a bank or commit financial suicide by sinking into a huge debt before you reap benefits. It's one of the businesses that many have succeeded in without owning property, securing a hefty loan, or putting down a huge down deposit. However, you still need to be savvy with your finances and plan around the budget so that you have a realistic guide that will help your business get off the ground.

With what you currently have, or where you currently are, what financial stance do you have? What are your business needs? What are the upfront costs that you're going to incur prior to setting up your business? These include the first trips or bookings you do as part of your market research. Any investment that you do—

including taking that seminar in a different city, or reading this book that is giving you all the inside info you need—towards this business counts as the upfront costs. Of course, these are not hefty expenses, but you need to include them in your budget so that you can settle them once the business is up and running.

Maybe your property needs renovations, a better wiring system, smart locks, new appliances, beds, the photographer, or anything that your business needs to make it listing-ready. How much money do you require upfront to set up your business? You will need to account for these before you can even start realizing any profits in your business. It is important to note that you separate the upfront costs from the running costs as they are usually once-off costs and easy to not consider them beforehand as part of the business expenses. Budget for them so that they don't dent your finances before you even open up shop.

Once you've considered what your business needs for it to be list-ready, it's time to consider what it will need as soon as you list it. This is where you list all your overheads and other running costs. Will you be cleaning the property yourself? What cleaning materials do you need on a daily basis? How much is your Wi-Fi subscription per month?

The Key Factors of a Good Business Plan

▷ **The Business Summary**

The executive summary entails your business overview. It should be done thoroughly to bundle your business idea and must include the summary of all the important details as this is the part investors spend the most time on. A good business summary shows investors that you have done your research and know what your business needs to get off ground and soar. Even if you don't intend to approach investors for your business, an executive summary serves as your compass to navigate your business journey. It's an overview of what you need to do and where to start; you can frequently review it to check how far you've come with your business.

The business summary is pretty much something that is addressed in the section above. It includes your mission statement, products and services, market research, budget, and team. It's a compelling piece of writing that serves as the business blueprint. Pay attention to think it through and write it down as precisely as possible. You can set an appointment with your financial advisor to discuss your business plan or outsource a company that can help you structure a compelling business plan, especially if you plan on using it to approach investors.

▷ The Company Description

This section here must include all key information about your business, emphasizing your goals, customer avatar, and the problem you want to solve. A compelling company description indicates that you know the details of your business, what distinguishes it from the rest, its strengths, the solution it offers, and its competitive edge. Show off to possible investors that your idea is truly yours by writing a comprehensive company description, indicating that you know the inception of your business and the direction it will take.

▷ The Market Analysis

Using the provided tools in Chapter 2, extract market analysis data to show that you have thoroughly thought through this business. A proper market research will give insight on the potential performance of your business based on the performance of competitive establishments in that area. It will also reveal that you know your targeted audience and have structured how you will make your business more appealing to them. Adding figures to this section of your business not only shows that you are realistic, but it will also appeal to your investors or landlords and will make you sound like an authority in this niche.

▷ **The Competitor Analysis**

Realistically, you are not the only Airbnb in your area. With the statistics that we've already shared, it is apparent that this niche is already overcrowded. However, just as every guest and host are unique, you can design to bring uniqueness in this business. A healthy competition exists so as to give you a nudge. Narrow down your direct and indirect competitors by looking into their abilities, taking advantage of their weaknesses while acknowledging their strengths.

▷ **Your Products and Services**

No one knows and can describe your services and products better than you, so this is your chance to shine in your business plan. Expand on the company description by detailing how your business is designed to operate. What services are you going to provide? What amenities are unique to your establishment? Who are your suppliers? Breakdown all the products and services you are going to offer and at which competitive prices.

▷ **Your Marketing Plan**

With the information you've already gathered, it shouldn't be hard to break down your marketing plan. Detail how you are going to ensure that your products and services reach your targeted audience. Which mediums of advertising are you going to use? How effective do they seem? For instance, if you're going to use billboards or guerrilla marketing, have you determined how many people will see your ad in a day? If it's a banner on a frequented tourism site, do you know how many visits the site has on a daily basis? Show that you already have a thorough idea of how effective your marketing plan will be.

▷ Your Sales Strategy

Slightly similar to the point above, your sales strategy will entail your intended action plans you will set in motion. How will you get people into your business? Will you give discounts to ensure that your occupancy rate stays up? Will you encourage referrals and reward them in order to have return guests? What strategies do you plan to rollout to have people choosing your property over that of your competition? What are your sales targets?

▷ Your Finances

This section is one of the most important ones in any business plan. Irrespective of whether or not you will use it to pitch to investors or for your own measurement of performance, finances are a clear indication of the profitability of a business. Breaking down your financial projections will show that you have thought through the costs of starting, operating, and maintaining your business. It will also show your anticipated revenue and return on investment, given the average occupancy rate. In this section, you also need to account for the cost of supplies, amenities, permit renewals, renovations, cleaning and maintenance staff, co-hosts, and management fees, as well as salaries.

Every dollar must be accounted for how it's intended to be used. Then you will be able to project feasible profits once all utilities, overheads, and other costs have been set aside. You will also be able to price your Airbnb for profit. If you are going to use rental arbitrage, property owners will definitely pay more attention on this part. The same is the case if you're going to apply for any form of financing. Spend as much time as possible to ensure that it's spectacular, and don't forget taxes!

THE LEGALITIES

The Rules, Regulations, and Laws

▷ **Step #1: Check the Rental Rules in Your City**

Depending on where you want your business to be located, there are some regulations that you need to consider prior to listing your property. Remember that if it's not done right, the Airbnb business can be illegal —and trust me, you don't want to be on the wrong side of the law. While it's possible to get correct information from different websites and from Airbnb gurus, some information can be falsified or omit important legal aspects. So irrespective of how you trust external sources, always confirm with your city or jurisdiction regulations what laws apply for short-term and long-term rentals. Even the Airbnb site specifies that regulations vary from county to county, state to state, or even country to country. It's paramount that you get the correct information regarding your specific intended business location.

▷ **Step #2: Obtain the Necessary Permit and Licenses**

• **Business Licenses**

The Airbnb marketplace emphasizes the need to follow proper channels that specifically apply to your area. Some jurisdictions require you to have a business license prior to operating. You need to contact your local government office to find out more on this, and also get necessary forms to fill your application, which usually is just a click of a website.

• **Building and Housing Standards**

This is one of the most important entries on your to-do list prior to commencing anything regarding your

Airbnb business. As we have already established, opening your home or property to host people means you inherit certain responsibilities towards the well-being of your guests. Your property may be subject to inspection in order to confirm that it meets certain habitability standards, that it is the right design, and that construction and maintenance standards are met. For instance, a property may be situated under a power line which poses a hazardous threat should there be any power fault. As a normal resident, you may not be aware of this; that is why it's important to call in the pros for these kinds of inspections. You also need to ensure that your property complies with the health and safety requirements, it is insured, and the security features are in place.

- **Zoning Rules**

Some properties may be subject to zoning laws which can be found in a zoning code, planning code, or city ordinances. The Airbnb marketplace requires that hosts contact their local government in order to verify that their property listings are consistent with the requirements. Steps to find what rules apply to your zone include visiting your county zoning webpage, finding the Geographical Information Systems (GIS) map, finding the land where your property is situated, checking the use table, and verifying what is allowed on that zone.

It helps to know about what zone laws apply to your jurisdiction so that you at least know that the property you have in mind—or already have—complies with the regulations. The key components that every zone has include a zone map, use tables, and standards. The zone map details the topography of an area in such a way that it shows the density of an area and the kind and size of infrastructure that can be built there. The use table pretty much entails what type of use cases a certain piece of land can be designated for; for example, a duplex, townhouse, restaurant, factory, or shopping mall would not occupy the same piece of land. Lastly, the standards detail the regulations and specifications of a property such as the building height, distance between units, and yard setbacks (Andrew, 2021).

- **Special Permit**

Well, having done a thorough research on the items above will give you a clear direction of the kind of permit your property needs for its intended establishment. Your city zoning ordinances have these files that you can study for yourself, or you can call the local government to confirm the kind of permit required for your establishment. The use table under zoning rules already specifies different levels of permissions certain establishments need. These range from permitted, conditional, or special permits. It's best that you start with checking the zoning regulations prior to calling for a special permit in case your establishment doesn't need it or to confirm the kind of permit it needs. It is advisable to do this way early in your preparations for your Airbnb business, preferably during the business planning so that if you need financing for your property, you get it for the right one that will allow you to operate your establishment (Andrew, 2021).

- **Landlord-Tenant Laws**

Depending on the duration of your hosting, you may be liable to comply with landlord-tenant laws. Some jurisdictions allow tenants who stay a certain number of days in your property to have certain rights that, if you are not aware of them, you may find it to be a hassle to evict them if you no longer wish to have them in your property. Squatters who know tenancy laws may refuse to leave your property after a certain period of days, and may even stay without paying rent if they know that you are not following proper eviction channels. During that squabble or legal battle, your property could be losing money. So, have a clear perspective of how you can be safe.

- **Taxes**

Tax laws may differ per jurisdiction; find out what your local government says about this. You may be required to collect taxes on a nightly basis or be exempted if you only lease your property for a limited number of days. In some jurisdictions, Airbnb may make things easier for you by collecting taxes and remitting them on your behalf. It's always wise to contact the relevant authority to determine what tax laws apply to you so that you're on the right side of the law.

▷ **Step #3: Check the Taxes and Their Rules**

As briefly mentioned above, you need to check tax rules that apply to your jurisdiction and ensure that you comply. Bear in mind that Airbnb will not automatically collect and remit taxes for all jurisdictions, so verify that you are collecting taxes if Airbnb is not doing it for you.

▷ **Step #4: Consider Safety and Insurance Regulations**

You need to ensure that you are up-to-date with safety regulations regarding your property. As much as Airbnb covers up to $1 million in the event that your property has been destroyed during a guest's stay, this does not cover everything. This means that there is a need to have your own insurance and read the fine print in order to know what you're covered for or not. You may be required by Airbnb to abide by the safety regulations, such as ensuring that the fire extinguisher is functional in case of emergencies.

▷ **Step #5: Avoid False Advertisement of Your Property**

Don't oversell your property or omit certain issues around it. Avoid fabricating lies to enhance the listing of your property with false information. You could get banned if the guest reports you on this to Airbnb. Let your property shine on merit and find its unique selling point without sensationalizing it.

TAXES

It is paramount to note that Airbnb is an income-generating business and thus you need to pay taxes. It's no secret that taxes are not a fun topic to discuss and they can be a little tricky. But, I aim to simplify taxes so that, like the wealthy, you know the legal hacks to go about getting your taxes reduced and exempted. This is not tax evasion which is illegal; it is a legitimate way of avoiding paying extortious amounts of money in taxes. The best advice about taxes is getting a great and licensed accountant who has your best interests at heart. Their job is to make sure that you don't naively give more money to the IRS than you have to. Because quite frankly, it's not just about how much money you make, but how much you keep.

Some of the best rental tax deductions you can take advantage of and avoid yearly tax burden include the following:

- *Qualified Business Income (QBI)*: This allows a pass-through income of up to 20% after deductions.
- *Depreciation*: Your property and other durable appliances also need to be accounted for and deducted yearly at this formula: (Purchase - value) / 27.5 years.
- *Travel expenses*: Any errands you do whether with your car; you can track your mileage and which the government allows a write-off to cover maintenance, gas, and depreciation of your car. Your abroad traveling in relation to your business can also be accounted for and qualify as a business expense that should be written-off; don't just travel for fun, but tie that to research or any conferences for your business.
- *Upgrades and maintenance*: Everything that you do to remodel your property is a tax write-off,

so you can use your Airbnb revenue to do upgrades, which will do even better for your property while getting that tax deduction.

- *Monthly expenses*: Mortgage, utilities, and any other supplies you paid for to make your guests feel more welcome are tax deductible (Andrew, 2020).

IRS Forms

There are a number of IRS forms you need to familiarize yourself with so that you know which one you need to fill out during your tax filing and reporting, depending on the type of establishment you have or your residential status. Whether you are earning an active (Schedule C) or passive (Schedule E) income through your property, you need to pay taxes if you rent out property for more than 14 days.

- Form 1099–k is used to report all card payments and third party network transactions if they exceed $200 and the gross payment is $20,000 and above.
- Form 1040 is used by every U.S. taxpayer to report an individual income tax return.
- Form 1042–s is used by foreign persons in the U.S to report source of income and is subject to withholding.

- Form W–8BEN is used as a certificate of foreign status beneficial owner and is also subject to withholding.
- Form 1099–NEC is used to report non-employee compensation (IRS, 2018).

KEY POINTS

- The business plan is the backbone of every successful business; pay attention to the mission statement, executive summary, and company description to set the tone for your Airbnb.
- Conducting a thorough marketing and competitor analysis will give you a clear picture of how your business is likely to perform and what pain points you need to focus on in order to be a cut above the rest.
- Be honest with your financial stance and be realistic with how much you anticipate as revenue minus the costs of your business so that you know if it will be worth it to run your operation from that intended location.
- Your financial forecast can help you with the pricing of your property and give you an indication of whether to pursue that business

the way you intended or whether you need to make adjustments.

- It is wise to know the legalities pertaining to operating Airbnb in your area. The local government or zoning ordinances will give you a clear direction of what permits you might need so that you stay on the right side of the law.
- You also need to comply with tax regulations; however, find ways to legally reduce what you pay to the IRS.

Whew! Now that you have the boring part of Airbnb out of the way, it's time to look at the fun side and prepare to make your listing the best possible place for your guest.

4

SPRUCING UP YOUR AIRBNB LOCATION

Now that the fine print that dragged the previous chapter is dealt with, let's look into the exciting part of Airbnb. Jazzing up your place so that it's the ideal and perfect choice for your guests can do wonders to your occupancy, finances, and reviews.

REASONS TO DECORATE YOUR HOME

Enhances Your Sales

People are drawn to energy, so your place must have a welcoming character that just makes guests want to be around. Taking time to adorn your place is like crafting an invitation letter with ego-boosting words that make the invitee feel wanted. It makes your guests feel your warm energy that is drawing them to share your space.

This is bound to enhance your sales. When you look into analytics, a home with an inviting character stands out from the rest of the dull ones, and the more it gets clicks, the more the search engines optimize it to the top results. Aesthetics are the first opportunity to lure and mesmerize someone to find reason to look into something. Knowing this will help you pay attention and ensure that the cover photo of your home is one that captures people's attention—your sales will skyrocket.

Gives the House a Fresh Start

There is something about a well-decorated home that shows the host is attentive to detail and makes the effort to keep things exciting. This is similar to having a clean space; it just refreshes the environment and makes the place look new. New things are exciting and our explorative selves can't help but be attracted to enjoy a fresh home. Decoration gives a house a revamped look that looks fresh and inviting.

Colors Can Change the Experience

Decorating a home does not have to involve adding expensive furniture or changing a lot of things. It can be a simple exercise like playing with colors. Painting the walls with a new color removes dullness—or that overly familiar look—into something fresh and new. Colors are not only artistic but they can playfully do wonders for an ordinary display. For instance, adding new cushions on a plain bedding set can give the illusion that even the bed is new. Adding fresh flowers, a colorful portrait, or changing curtains and pillowcases can change the entire living space without breaking your budget.

Making Use of Extra Space

Another underrated method of decorating is decluttering. One thing about intentionally revamping your place is that you will identify items that have overstayed their welcome and need to be removed or shifted. There is something refreshing about a minimalist look. It makes the place look more spacious, tidy, and accommodative. Take advantage of shifting things around; remove those the space can do without and be creative with the newly created space. Remember that guests bring their own personal items and a minimalist look portrays that the space can accommodate them.

THE AMENITIES

Amenities are fantastic enticements to draw guests to your place. There is something about leaving your home to go into another that has what your home has or more. I mean, one of the main reasons hotels keep adding amenities like Jacuzzis, saunas, or gymnasiums is because guests want something that can entertain them while they are away from their homes. Unlike with some hotels that have standard amenities, Airbnb amenities can be more exciting as they reflect the personality of the host and show how hospitable they are.

The reason we emphasized on conducting market research is so that you know what guests want in order to be able to offer it to them before they even ask. The key is to provide amenities that make a guest feel taken care of, and doing this includes adding things that people may even have forgotten they might need while they are away from their homes. This makes you a thoughtful host who understands what your guests want. Some amenities go beyond entertainment and we'll briefly discuss different amenities below.

The Most Common Amenities

These amenities listed below are not really essential, but guests appreciate them. For instance, having a pet-friendly home will attract guests that have and love to travel with their furry friends and family, opting for your property over a hotel or other hosts that do not accommodate pets. It's not a must to have this, but it sure does make your listing stand out to the guests who own pets—and those with children know that your place might be child-friendly. The same applies for Wi-Fi, extra adapters, or working space; it's not essential, but it will attract business travelers.

- A pet-friendly home
- Wi-Fi
- Parking
- Swimming pool
- Jacuzzi
- Kitchen
- Air conditioning
- Heating
- Washer and dryer
- TV and Netflix

Essential Amenities

There are standard and essential amenities that can be found in almost every Airbnb, and they may include but are not limited to:

- One clean bath towel per guest
- One hand towel by the vanity
- One pillow per guest
- Fresh linens for each bed
- Body wash, shampoo, or soap bar
- Toilet paper
- Disinfectant wipes or spray
- Antibacterial hand sanitizer
- Multi-surface cleaner and gloves

Safety Amenities

- The smoke alarm
- Carbon monoxide alarm
- Fire extinguisher
- First aid kit
- Emergency plan and local numbers (ambulance, police, ambassador, or any authorities)

THE DECORATIONS

Decorating your Airbnb is not only a fun thing to do, but it will do wonders to draw people to your property as well as separate your place from a cookie cutter hotel theme. It's exciting for both the host and the guest to walk into a room or house that has its own unique statement.

How to Decorate Your Airbnb

▷ **Know Your Guests**

Bear in mind who your ideal guest is so that the place is appealing to them. If you want to attract business travelers, having a large working desk with a couple of books here and there, one or two quote frames or artwork, and minimal frills is a thumbs up. A backpacker or group of travelers may appreciate your effort with a beanbag, comfortable couch, and enough sleep area. Parents would be attracted to a colorful place. Know who your ideal guest is and design your decor with them in mind.

▷ **Go For Consistent Themes**

Pleasing everyone can be hard and impossible. Try to go for themes that are consistent and not seasonal. Yes, during different seasons you can spruce up your place to go with the theme, but only on things that are easy to move, like cushions and vases. Go for natural colors and nude palettes to be safe. Select at least one focal point that can be a solid color that is complemented by the rest of the add-ons.

Decorating Tips

- Pay attention to colors.
- Experiment with textures and patterns.
- Make sure it stays clean by covering up sensitive colors on fabrics.
- Don't overspend; think of creative and affordable ways to adorn your place.
- Go for a minimalist look and pay attention to detail.

KEY POINTS

- Consider your guests when you design your amenities list.
- Make sure that your place attracts your ideal guest.
- Pay attention to details when decorating your place.

- Go for consistent themes to accommodate
  more people.

Which of these amenities categories appeal more
to you?

- Luxury
- Basic / Essential
- Safety
- Family
- Couple
- Business

5

GETTING ON THE AIRBNB PLATFORM

There are no strangers here, only friends you haven't yet met.

— WILLIAM BUTLER YEATS

CREATING YOUR HOST PROFILE

In his TED talk, one of the founders of Airbnb, Joe Gebbia, described how we've been indoctrinated that we should stay away from strangers, and he wondered: What if strangers are just friends waiting to happen? How many opportunities to meet incredible people have we let pass? When starting this business, Gebbia and his co-founder friends realized that it needs trust, which can be a difficult thing when people don't know anything about each other. This works both ways with hosts and guests. Just as much as you can be skeptical to accept a booking from a faceless profile, guests are not so keen to click on listings that share no personal details of the host. Airbnb founders also knew from their design and engineering background that any business can be designed for trust, which is how they structured the business model in such a way that people know they can rely on it.

People feel safer to work with someone whose identity has been vetted. Your profile is your first opportunity to let people know more about you. It's important that you fill it as honestly as possible. Airbnb requires verifications of every user of the marketplace so that all parties are protected. Moreover, the main thing as host is that your profile is there to sell your property, so make sure that it attracts clicks, because what good is it if it gets no clicks?

Describing Yourself on Airbnb

So how do you appeal to your potential guests? Your name is probably the first thing towards allowing people to know who you are. Share your real name so that at least people know what to call you. When someone knows who you are, the strange feeling of a mysterious identity is removed. The next step to introduce yourself is to share where you are from. Disclosing where you are from is an invitation on its own, as it's an important aspect about your origin, location, or where you are based. If you're in the same location with your property, it's also a way to share your listing, although your property listing details are separate from your personal profile. You can take a step further to introducing yourself by sharing the kind of work you do as well as your hobbies. Including your favorite travel destinations also shows people that you are explorative, which is one thing you have in common. It also shows that you love being a guest at some point—or you have been a guest—which makes you a reliable person to offer hospitality based on your experience.

Upload a Great Profile Picture

Your profile picture says a lot about you, so take careful attention to it. It must be high quality, not pixelated or blurred. Ensure that your picture is a headshot so that your features are visible for an easy, near eye contact experience with the end user. People can sense your energy from your picture, so show that smile which will let people know that you are approachable. You also need to look presentable to show that you took the effort to look professional and friendly at the same time. A key to taking a great picture is by being yourself; this means you also need to be and look comfortable.

Verify Your Airbnb Profile

You've already shared a little about yourself, but you can seal this by verifying your profile so that people know the person on the profile does exist in real life. By providing your identity verification, you help Airbnb keep the trust in the community and you're likely going to come off as reliable and trustworthy. To verify your identity, you need to upload a clear copy of your ID, be it driver's license or passport. You also need to verify your email address and phone number to show that you'll be able to receive any notifications and your communication channels are working.

Add Some References

Previous references from some people you've worked with or past experience in a similar industry boosts reliability and proves credibility. That is why going forward, reviews are an important aspect that proves to guests they can stay at your property and be safe and well-accommodated.

CREATING YOUR LISTING

The Perfect Title

The job of the title or heading of your listing is to capture someone's attention and lure them to read the first line. Make sure your title is catchy, unique, brief, and memorable. A good title appeals to your ideal client and invites them to want to know more while hinting at an important aspect that is your unique selling point. It can either describe a location, spark intrigue, answer a question, or address a pain. For instance, phrases like "stunning view of the scenic mountains" or "stone's throw from the beach" describe your property location based on fun things around it.

To spark intrigue, you can use any mystic words that provoke one's curiosity about your property. Bear in mind that you only have 50 characters to fit your title, so avoid generic, filler words and maximize the use of those limited characters to show enough detail to capture guest attention. In order to do this, your title needs to address a certain group of people only, not accommodating everyone. This means you must know your guest avatar and be able to promise a fulfillment of their wishes.

Whether it's people who are nature lovers, business travelers, pet owners, or a family with kids, try to give them what they desire without them even asking. If you want to attract guests who are big spenders, words like 'luxury' or 'exquisite' might appeal to them, while 'perfectly-priced,' "on a budget," "ideal for backpackers," or 'affordable' will attract travelers who are minimalist and like to save every penny. Phrases like "perfect love nest, cozy and secluded oasis" will surely attract couples while 'pet-friendly' or 'child-friendly' will appeal to families.

Use abbreviated words that are simple to guess, for instance: AC for air conditioner or w/ for with. You can also use symbols and emojis to convey information in your title, like the plane emoji to indicate that you're near the airport. Don't overdo it with symbols to avoid loss of meaning; limit them to less than a handful. Use title case instead of all caps in your title. Highlight your best features, upgrades, or anything that summarizes the experience as revealed by the reviews.

The Perfect Description

The description is there to expand on the title to elaborate more on your amenities. You can address concerns like safety by highlighting things, like how secure the neighborhood is to take quiet night strolls to and from a certain attraction point. Describing your comfy bed with "orthopedic, queen, and turn-free mattress" will attract people looking for a peaceful night rest, or "spacious living room with extra sleepers" if your target is not a solo traveler. "A dash to the convenient store, shopping mall, or pharmacy" answers the concern that in case of an emergency, the guest will have their immediate needs catered for within minutes. Lightning-fast Wi-Fi is a big attraction for business travelers.

Make use of adjectives to enhance your property; make it stand out from ordinary services or amenities by other hosts. Just as you were specific with the title, address your ideal guest by mentioning why your place is the perfect spot for what they may get up to. Mentioning that the property has a remote-controlled gate and garage sounds convenient to car owners. Don't forget to share the experience of the local attraction, landmark, or anything worth mentioning in your vicinity so that guests know there are plenty of fun things to do during their stay. Describe the experience with phrases that paint the location or event with 'not-to-be-missed' kinds of vibes.

Be specific about the distance, ambience, or safety of the route to a local hangout spot, landmark, or anything relevant. However, try not to oversell the property with fabricated information, as this will lead to a terrible set of reviews by guests who made the effort to travel for that hyped experience only to be disappointed. Write your description and read it out loud to analyze if it's something that would call you to experience it. Take time to describe your listing and edit it over time as you add more amenities. Pay attention to what guests rave about in reviews, take their suggestions to heart, and incorporate changes to offer the best guest experience.

The Perfect Photos

Between the listing title and the cover photo of your Airbnb, you have the first opportunity to grab your target audience's attention; therefore, you must put in more effort to perfect these sections. The first picture that is displayed on your listing must be your best shot of all the photos in the reel.

The mistake that most hosts make is taking multiple pictures that serve no purpose. Just because there is no specified number of pictures allowed does not mean the host must create a busy gallery with repeat photos showing the same angle. Remember that it's quality over quantity, so even a small number of photos can do wonders as long as they reflect the best parts of your property and all the necessary amenities (Jasper, 2019).

▷ **Declutter Your Space**

The minimalist look has a way of showcasing a property in an elegant, neat, and spacious manner. Clean every room thoroughly. For the pictures meant to sell your business to the world, don't skimp trying to save costs. Get the property professionally cleaned and free of any personal clutter.

▷ **Lighting**

Lighting enhances the look of a photo, so try to get as much natural light as possible and turn on the lights when you take photos. Avoid direct sunlight as it can over-brighten pictures and ruin the contrast.

▷ **Angles**

Take photos from different angles to show the room at large. Corner angles are perfect to show two or three walls of the house in one setting. Pay attention to detail, especially with your best amenities. Show the full size of the bed in your photos. Also, consider panoramic shots. Show your Airbnb lifestyle and its character in your photos. Take it to the next level and add shots of your neighborhood.

KEY POINTS

- Some proven best formulas involve playing around with adjectives, property type, key features, and distance from landmarks.
- A well-executed description paints a vivid picture of the location, property, and experience, even without looking at the pictures.
- Invest in quality photos and a professionally cleaned house that is free from clutter prior to taking photos.
- Display your best amenities in the photo reels and show nearby attractions.

6

MARKETING AND SCALING YOUR BUSINESS

Stopping advertising to save money is like stopping your watch to save time.

— HENRY FORD

ADVERTISING YOUR PROPERTY

Marketing Tips for Airbnb

You have done an incredible job setting up your profile on the platform. While this means that your listing is live and visible to existing Airbnb users, it is your responsibility to drive traffic towards the site. Some people in your area or anywhere in the world may not be aware of your listing if they are not on Airbnb. You can take marketing further and take to external marketplaces to let people know of your business and make them aware of the Airbnb services.

▷ Use Social Media

About 58.4% of the world's population is active on social media, with a significant growth tracked back to new users coming into the digital world within the past 12 months (Chaffey, 2020). More than half of the global population have increased the average person's social media time to over two hours, so it makes sense to use social media to boost your Airbnb business. Social media platforms are full of the latest trends in almost everything from lifestyle, food, entertainment, and travel. It's true that the hospitality business might have taken a knock when the global pandemic hit, but social media kept people and companies entertained. People shared their old travel moments, things that they would like to do post-travel restrictions, and iconic places even started hosting virtual events on social media.

Not everyone might have Airbnb platforms, which limits the number of people exposed to your listing to the users of the platform. However, you can go where people are gathered on these social pages and share your Airbnb listing there. The trick is to make it fun and engaging just as social media content is. You can share stories, reels, or any visual media of your property with interesting captions and attach the link that will redirect clicks to your Airbnb listing. If you're not an expert with social media, you may want to consider hiring a social media manager or content creator that will curate your property media in a way that will attract clicks.

With tools like Instagram reels, stories, and TikTok videos, the nice thing is that your content gets to be shown to millions of people even if they are not following you. This is why it must be engaging and interactive so that you build a following from those platforms and generate leads to your listing. Social media thrives on aesthetics; that is why getting beautiful photos of your interior furnishings and curated amenities will do wonders getting leads to your pages.

▷ **Create a Unique URL for Your Airbnb Listing**

Promoting your Airbnb listing requires you to have a little creativity to find angles in which you can customize it. You can use easy-to-remember keywords that portray your listing better than a long alphanumeric link that people might be skeptical to click. You can also ensure that your link shows a great thumbnail that lures people to click. The more clicks you get, the better traffic to your listing, and the more your visibility on search engines improves.

▷ Work With a Blogger

Most bloggers have enormous experience with social media and a massive following. Any piece they share about your property can do you a lot of good. While this might not come cheap, it could be the best investment in the long run, considering that bloggers already have loyal followers who trust their recommendations. You can work with a blogger from a paid angle where you can get a full feature on her blog, or you can work from a collaborative angle. In order to grab their attention, you would have to make them an offer they cannot refuse, like inviting them to stay at your property for free for a special occasion and, in turn, they write a feature on their experience. Even if they don't write a full feature, just posting about being at your establishment with aesthetic pictures is bound to get tongues wagging.

A pro-tip when selecting a blogger to partner with for your feature is to get one with at least basic copywriting skills, as they will embed keywords and tags that will optimize your feature to be top in the search engine results. You also have to have a great establishment already so that you're not overhyped by the article only to be below average when guests that follow the blog decide to try your property. This means that you should have already bagged some great reviews and a good reputation for your place. It would help if you do this when you are ready for more responsibilities as you need to be able to handle the influx that will come with this publicity.

▷ Find Traveling Forums Online

Consider becoming part of an online traveling or vacation rental forum where you can network with other like-minded people. This will help you stay informed about the trends in your industry and you will know if there are upcoming events that you can prepare for. There is so much to learn by belonging to a forum where travel and vacation rentals are a hot topic, from how other hosts handle certain situations to new tips on how to improve your business. Participating by sharing your ideas in the forum will also position you as a force with credibility, and fellow hosts might send some business your way knowing that you are reliable.

▷ Get Listed on Local Tourism Websites

Find a way to approach the local tourism site and ask to be listed on their website and informational pamphlets. As a listed service provider on trusted sites like these, you will expose your business to out-of-town guests who are visiting the area. With this way of announcing your services to the community, your tourism board might also consider you when they have special events and invite you for networking sessions which will surely boost your bookings.

▷ Promotional Flyers and Business Cards

Despite the exponential growth in digital media, do not underestimate the power that print media still holds. Some people still prefer hard copies, so consider having flyers that showcase your property, amenities, and contacts; then, share these publicly. You can also ask your local newspaper or stores to include them when they mail their promotional paper in your neighborhood or suburb. Since your guests will also be using local restaurants, bars, and other convenient stores in your area, don't be shy to ask these places if you can leave your flyers there or if you can place your poster on their notice boards. Business cards are great to have so you can share them when attending forums, events, or even traveling. By extending invitations in person to guests to stay at your place when they are in your area, you're already showing them what a hospitable host you are by creating a deeper connection, thus improving your chances to get booked.

▷ Consider Discounts for Your Customers

Show your customers that you love having them around by creating special offers for them. You can put appealing discounts when they schedule their next stay or when they refer guests to you. If you want to take this connection to a higher level, you can even send special messages on their birthdays and offer them promotional codes that they can use on their next stay. Not only will your personalized message make them feel remembered on their special days, it will also remind them of the great time they had during their stay. Who knows? This might be the greatest way to appeal to guests so that they return or even have a new tradition to visit your place whenever they want to unwind.

▷ Have an Emailing List

An emailing list is one of the oldest methods for direct marketing that is still profitable today. You need to find a way to collect customer contact details so that you can add them to your database for future reference. You can use the mailing list to inform your guests of upcoming promotions, exciting events that are happening in your area, or to send birthday messages as indicated above. Airbnb allows sharing of contact information once the booking has already been made, so you can get guests' emails by suggesting to send some material related to their booking. This could be some itinerary or any travel guide to familiarize themselves with prior to their arrival.

Try to avoid being spammy with multiple emails and only use this option when necessary, bearing in mind that it's also an expense. Monitor from your analytics if the unsubscribe list is growing to decide if this is working for you or not. This way, not only does Airbnb own their clients, but you also own your clients. Owning your clients is a safety precaution and forward thinking for those rare occasions when one terrible review can have your account banned from the entire site (STR University, 2019).

▷ Take Advantage of Google Maps

Many people use Google Maps for navigating around areas. You can have a location pin embedded on Google Maps by giving details of your address and naming your property to claim that pin as yours. That way, it's easier for clients to access and it also improves your property visibility on Google search.

▷ Send Photos of Your Airbnb to Design Blogs

Depending on your angle, you can find appealing ways to approach interior design blogs or real estate magazines with fresh content. Maybe you've just bought a new item like any smart gadget that does something ordinary in a unique way; send photos of it to them and see if they might be interested in featuring your property.

Tools to Use for Your Airbnb

With the way the Airbnb business has evolved over the years, there are tools that you can use to boost your listing to different platforms that will still redirect to your property, giving your listing more visibility. Listing your property on multiple channels is a great way to increase your bookings. However, without the right management tools, hosts have to manually update their calendars on all booking channels, which can be a huge waste of time. Manual calendar updates also introduce a high risk of double bookings during the updating process, and this may lead to canceling of guests, which is a terrible thing if you're gunning for the superhost status or you want to maintain it.

▷ **Hosthub**

Formerly known as Syncbnb, Hosthub is a property management tool that helps synchronize your bookings calendar over multiple channels so that you can avoid double bookings. Whether you've listed your property on Booking.com, TripAdvisor, VRBO, or any other marketplace, Hosthub tracks your bookings automatically such that when your listing has been booked on one platform, those dates are updated on other channels as occupied (Hosthub, 2018).

▷ **Hospitable**

Hospitable is vacation rental software similar to Hosthub; it was formerly known as SmartBNB and is used for automation. This awesome tool is able to be programmed in your preferred—and more personal—tone as it automatically responds to messages. Hospitable is also able to send personalized reviews which you can send instantly or edit before you send. With tools like this one, your communication and response rate is bound to go up, thereby increasing your algorithms for Airbnb and SEO (The Fearless Investor, 2020).

▷ **Furnished Finder**

Furnished Finder is another incredible marketplace for short term rentals. It specializes in connecting travel nurses to furnished home owners that are looking for short term tenants for their property. Furnished Finder differs from Airbnb with a number of details like fees and management. Airbnb takes 3% fees on every booking while Furnished Finder hosts pay a flat fee of only $99 per year. Airbnb handles a lot of managing for the host as it takes care of the leases, insurance, and payments, while Furnished Finder does not do these for the users but directly links the property owner with the tenant to reach their own lease agreement privately. It has, however, partnered with third parties like

KeyCheck where users are verified and payments can be safely made.

Furnished Finder is a great tool or marketplace to list your property with no strings attached, as you do the guest screening yourself and decide which tenants to accept. It's also considered to be easy to start and manage, provided you're willing to risk the investment of $99 upfront fee; then, it advertises your property to the relevant guests who need your services. Furnished Finder is however yet to make its mark in the real estate and vacation rentals space, which leaves you with a choice to either go with the more experienced Airbnb marketplace or try out Furnished Finder which is also growing at an exponential rate. If you want to use your property for long-term stays for travel nurses, Furnished Finder is your best bet, but for short vacation rentals, Airbnb and VRBO remain the preferred choice for hosts (Cassie Villela, Realtor - Silverbridge Realty, 2021).

When comparing Airbnb with Furnished Finder, a host who uses both business models looked at the start-up cost, difficulty to manage, scaling opportunities, and earning potential. Airbnb may take up much resources to set it up as you have to impress clients for it to be booked and receive great reviews, while Furnished Finder entails looking at the property, furnishing it, and listing it on the marketplace that is already saturated with nurses that request accommodation. In terms of difficulty, the user mentioned that Airbnb entails more work as it needs to be cleaned or maintained frequently after every guest checks out, which is not the case with Furnished Finder where the one tenant can stay for longer with little to no maintenance required during their stay. Airbnb, however, scales more as most of its management can be automated, leaving the host more freedom to look for more property, and it brings in more money depending on the occupancy rate.

From these comparisons, it can be concluded that both models can work parallel to each other, depending on what you find manageable. It is important to note that these two fall into different categories: the hospitality business, which is more intimate and demanding to ensure that guests have a better experience, and the real estate business, through landlord-tenant relationships. At the end of the day, it's your property and your rules, so you can list the same property with both Airbnb and Furnished Finder. There is no risk of double booking in this case as you have to vet your tenant before you approve them, during which you can update your calendar accordingly (Pimentel, 2021).

▷ Booking.com

Another popular marketplace where you can list your property is Booking.com. In terms of traffic, Booking.com is a clear winner as it is more widely searched and used by over 200 billion people than Airbnb. However, you can use this tool to enhance the visibility of your Airbnb; just bear in mind the charges, as Booking.com tends to charge way more than the 3% standard commission per booking that Airbnb does. With a great calendar sync in place, you will not face a double booking situation when you've listed your property on both marketplaces.

Marketing Strategies

▷ Create Your Brand

In order to take your Airbnb business to the next level, you need to consider branding. Branding helps set apart your business as it decouples from the rest of the similar businesses. It also makes the name or slogan of your business easy to remember—think banners, face boards, branded towels, business cards, and brochures. There's a reason why people check-in when they are at the Marriott or Hilton.

Branding your business indicates that you're in the business for the long run and you run a professional establishment—and that will draw more bookings. Look at how restaurants and fast food establishments take branding seriously. From the packaging, napkins, mints, and the places themselves, there is uniformity; wherever their clientele goes holding any branded item, it's extended marketing. When your guests arrive at your branded Airbnb, it no longer feels like an ordinary home, but it makes one feel like they're in a fancy hotel where they are allowed to live like they would in their own homes.

As you expand your business from that spare room to multi-homes and several properties in different locations, branding will help your guests identify and choose your establishment. Branding can help your business become a household name in no time. Think of simplicity, meaning, and noteworthiness when you brand your business.

▷ **Advertise With Social Media**

A business that is not on social media is truly living in the past. There's a plethora of opportunities that come with being out there where your clientele is flocking. An average person spends at least two hours a day on social media. You need to find a way for your post to reach them. Whether it's on Facebook, YouTube, or

TikTok, take your business where your market is saturated and bring them to your establishment. Travel bloggers share their content on social media and it has proved to bring massive traffic to their blogs. Social media platforms are a great place to generate leads for your listing.

You can either go with organic traffic or paid ads; as long as you're intentional about going global with your business, social media is the perfect vehicle. Millions of people are on Facebook, Instagram, Twitter, YouTube, and TikTok. With Facebook, Instagram, and WhatsApp, you can share the same content across these platforms by linking them to save time. Facebook has held many virtual tours of iconic museums, palaces, and other dreamy destinations. With stories, reels, and spaces, you get a chance to showcase your content to people who are not even your friends or followers. Your listing can go viral by sharing it or parts of it on social media platforms.

Social media platforms also have customizable parameters that you can use to send your message to relevant markets. With sponsored ads, you get to choose regions, age groups, and any criteria you want to use to narrow or widen your reach to your targeted audience. Take advantage of trending hashtags and add those relevant to your content. You may want to work with a professional content creator to package your message in such a manner that it appeals to your desired clientele.

▷ Create a Promotional Video

Just as you took a professional angle to get breathtaking pictures of your listing, you can prepare a promotional video that features your property, operations, and embed fun things to do. If your listing is just on the marketplace, it really is just there, static, but serving a purpose as it shows on the searches. However, you can take this to another level by bringing your property to life through videos.

▷ Collaborations

The hospitality industry is one of the easiest industries to create meaningful collaborations with other key players. You have the place, you can find crowd pullers, and you can make a deal to accommodate them freely in tandem to promoting your business. For instance, you can host lifestyle bloggers or influencers and they share their experience to their audience. You can have content creators use your facilities to produce their content in exchange for giving your place credit. You can collaborate with some suppliers so that you exclusively use their branded products for your guests.

▷ **Find Some Local Partnerships**

Experience is one of the exciting parts of Airbnb, so plan to make your guests' stay memorable and enhance your listing by partnering with local hangouts. You can make a deal with local places where every time you bring a guest they get a discount or an extra item courtesy of your partnership. Guests will feel taken care of and your partners will also bring business your way.

▷ **Use SEO**

Search engine optimization is a proven method to reach the masses. Hire a copywriter or read well-written SEO articles to learn the tricks of using popularly searched keywords that will make your listing show on the top of the search results. Use sale-triggering phrases that will bait customers to click on your article. Not only will this drive traffic to your site, but it will also boost your algorithm so that your listing is optimized whenever people search anything relating to your property. Use Google AdWords, local travel sites, as well as vacation booking sites to generate leads to your listing.

THE SCALING

Scaling entails moving your business from average to the next level, becoming a mogul. Although you may want to start with an extra room in your home, the goal here is to go beyond owning one or two houses listed on Airbnb. This is where you have income from over a handful of properties. How do you achieve that without any property? I'm thrilled that you asked. This section is going to unbundle how to hack the system so that you earn from multiple properties, even if you don't own any. There are two main modes to scaling this business: through rental arbitrage and property management.

Rental Arbitrage

Rental arbitrage is a phenomenal real estate strategy similar to house hacking—the practice of introducing one to the real estate investment business by buying a home and renting out a portion of it in order to get used to being a landlord through learning-by-doing. With both rental arbitrage and house hacking, the rent paid by the tenant is used to offset the long-term mortgage. However, with rental arbitrage, you don't own the property; instead, you take a long-term lease with a landlord and sublet it on short-term rental platforms like Airbnb and VRBO. With this strategy, you can take out a number of leases with different landlords, get their permission to list their property on Airbnb, then use the income to pay your rent—you can either pay a surcharged rent or share Airbnb profits with your landlord—and invest your profits in the business (Jasper, 2019a).

The short-term rent can accumulate into a larger figure than you would need on a monthly payment plan and thus makes more profit. Therefore, rental arbitrage can be simplified as the way of using short-term rental income to settle a long-term rent. Rental arbitrage is the next level, game-changing way to scale your Airbnb business without the responsibility of owning any property. You can have as many leases as you want and put the rental units on Airbnb, where you can manage them through automation, co-hosting, or property management services.

Property Management

Another great way to start making money without capital is by becoming a property manager. To become a property manager means that you handle most of the responsibilities of the property owners. Co-hosts may fall into this category. As a PM, your duties go beyond using just Airbnb, as your job is to ensure that the properties you're managing generate income, meaning you can list properties on as many platforms as you wish.

Tips to Scale

- Listen to customer feedback.
- Develop a pricing plan.
- Aim for long-term bookings.
- Give customer incentives.

Use Airbnb Tools

There are numerous tools that you can incorporate in your day-to-day business that automate your communication and ensure that your business operates like a well-oiled machine.

- Peerspace is a great marketplace that ensures the end user has updated information on the space booked and requires that community guidelines are adhered to.
- Dropbox and Google Drive are perfect for easy sharing of files.
- Beyond Pricing is a great AirDNA tool to optimize your pricing strategy.
- SmartBNB and iGMS will help you automate most tasks as these tools work like PMS.
- AirDNA is an incredible weapon to use to launch a successful business, knowing sensitive information even about your competitors.

- WhatsApp for business is a free-to-use, great messaging tool that displays your catalog and allows you to send quick responses.

KEY POINTS

- The success of your business relies on great and intentional marketing. Strive to make your brand known by partnering with influencers and using social media.
- Optimize your listing visibility with other marketplaces.
- Take your business to the next level by using rental arbitrage and property management services to scale at no cost to you.
- Improve your communication and running of the business through automation.

7

WELCOMING YOUR FIRST GUEST

First impressions last when it comes to customer service. Even if you may do great things later in someone's life, they will not forget if you have made them feel bad in any way upon their first encounter with you. From what customers first see on your listing to when they arrive at your property, make it a great memory that represents your brand well.

THE STEPS TO WELCOMING A GUEST

Step #1: The Importance of Communication

In the hospitality industry, communication is the first step that showcases a warm reception of guests. Even prior to arriving at your property, ensure that your guests know you are eager to meet them, look out for them, and ensure that their needs are taken care of. In most cases, guests are coming to your area for the first time, making you the only familiar person about that place. Use this to your advantage in order to make your guests feel safe, knowing that you are looking out for them.

▷ Honesty Is the Best Policy

During the booking process, it is possible that guests may have forgotten some of the details about your place. Communicate with them frequently, ensuring that you remind them of those details that you feel you need to emphasize. Maybe getting to your place using public transport is slightly difficult; suggest alternative modes, like use of Uber, or ask if they would like to be picked up—it doesn't have to be for free, unless you are really close to their arrival point—or whatever suggestion you might have. Is the alarm system working? If not, communicate this ahead of time so they know that they have to call you or anyone managing the property upon arrival so they are not agitated when they arrive at a locked gate.

Maybe you need to remind them of other important details they might have missed that could have changed or need updating. Confirm or remind them of your pet policy, whether you allow pets or not. Let them also know what to expect when they arrive at your property. You don't have to go into detailed house rules yet, but communicate honestly with them. If there will be load-shedding or a temporary power outage around the time that they are arriving, let them know the electronic motor may not be functioning so that they are prepared to be patient as the gate is opened manually. Whatever you need to clear out prior to finally seeing them face-to-face, be honest and communicate it.

▷ Reply Promptly

Guests do not like waiting for their messages to be replied to, so avoid making them feel agitated by promptly responding to their messages through the Airbnb messaging feature or the app that notifies you when you receive messages and if you still have not responded. Using the app or message feature is good because you don't have to be on the platform for you to see and respond to messages; even if you've gone out on an errand, you're still available for your guest. As soon as you're able to, let your guest know that you are reachable by mobile or via text. Another way you can have efficient communication is through quick replies, especially if you're communicating with more than one client. Think ahead and set up generic responses for generic queries.

Step #2: Make the Check-In and Checkout Easy

From your communication, you should have established their estimated time of arrival by now. I know that you've specified check-in times, but find out when your guest is arriving in your area so that they are not wandering around with their luggage waiting for the actual time to check in. What will make you even more accommodative is being flexible with your check-in time. Let them know that they are allowed to come to the property to leave their luggage while you get their space ready. You want to go out of your way to make them feel welcome and safe in your area. Answer as many questions as possible and set yourself apart as the go-to person for anything they might need information on.

Upon the arrival of your guest, you—or someone you've stationed—need to be ready to open the gate for them with a smile. They must feel like they are a part of your family, so that genuine smile is a great first impression and a lasting memory of your reception. Greet them vibrantly and ask how their flight, drive, or journey was. Ask to help them carry their bags into the property and show them in. As you show them around, tell them how everything works, from how to operate the gate should they want to get out soon after checkout. If there's anything you must reiterate, you can do that in person—things like which water to use for the kettle if you have well water or municipal water separately.

Put all the important instructions on the information guide that the guests will find in the living room or on the coffee table. This guide also includes the Wi-Fi passcode, instructions on how to set up a lock should they need to reset it, your number to reach you upon any emergency, and basic house rules. The information guide should also contain other emergency help lines like the ambulance, fire department, hospital, and nearest police station. If you want, you can include the following on the same booklet or make a separate one: directions to the local store, pharmacy, hangouts, or any attractions in the vicinity. Some guests appreciate you sharing your favorite places to go; it makes them feel closer to you, and they are likely to try your suggestions.

Step #3: Make Everything Clean and Tidy

There is something welcoming and inviting about a clean space. Don't cut corners where the hygiene of your property is concerned. Pay attention to fine details to ensure that there are no specks of dust, stains, hairs, or anything that can turn off guests. Even if you've had another guest who checked out that day, let there be no evidence of prior occupancy. There should be no residual mess that proves the presence of the previous guest. Your place must look neat and fresh. Doing this sends a subtle message to your guest that they must keep things tidy and respect your property.

Consider hiring professional cleaning services for your property to ensure that everything is spick and span. Besides being trained to pay attention to detail, they will also not take things as personally as you do when they have to clean up after someone. If you see stains all over the bathroom, sheets, or towels, you might lose it, whereas the professional cleaners know that some stains will just need bleach or stain remover to restore the condition of an item. If you try to clean yourself, there are a lot of things that you might omit, which can be a turnoff upon guest arrival. Some hosts end up hating their business because it feels like a chore instead of something fun because they want to do things themselves. This makes them see the not-so-pretty side of the business and even feel that guests have no respect for their property. Having a professional do stuff like cleaning is the best way to go because there is no sentimental attachment to the place; they just take care of the mess and tidy up for the next guest without feeling offended (As Within Algenay, 2021).

Declutter the space of any of your personal belongings like photos, vases, or any notebooks so that guests cannot feel cramped up into your life. Sure, you can leave decorative portraits to make the house homey or have some magazines or books around for aesthetics. Depending on the duration of the stay of your guest, ensure that your house is well-stocked for the essentials. Include the cleaning supplies as well so that guests know they should clean up after themselves. It doesn't matter whether there's a cleaning fee they've paid or not; having enough cleaning supplies around encourages one to tidy up any visible mess. A neat look is a way to show guests that you want them to have a peaceful time in your home.

Step #4: Ensure That Their Needs Are Met

▷ **Stock up on the Essentials**

You have to anticipate what your guests might need upon arrival and ensure that you meet that need. The essential amenities like fresh towels, linens, soap, and toilet paper are a no brainer. Stock up your place with these essentials and let guests know that you've stocked up for the duration of their stay; that way, you avoid any wasteful use of your supplies. You can have extras like blankets should they feel cold, an extra pair of sheets should there be any accident—you don't want them to have to wait for the sheets to dry if they've washed them, and you also don't want to be called for things like these —let them handle it themselves without much of a hassle. Things like toilet paper and paper towels also have to be enough; maybe you can limit the ones that you display but have extras in the cabinets for when they run out.

Besides providing essential amenities and welcome goodies, some hosts suggest that you stock up on things that guests need to pay for should they use them— things like soft drinks, extra water, or any snacks that you have can be put separately, with a list that they should fill for things that need to be restocked. In this manner, you've taken care of the needs of your guests while also preventing any waste of your supplies.

▷ **Item Labeling**

Do not assume that guests will use your property exactly the same way that you do. One guest might be more considerate than the other. Ensure that you make things easier for your guests and save yourself from trouble by labeling your items. Things like instructions on how to use your appliances—water for the kettle or coffee maker should be different from drinking, or bathing water if you have a water hole—should go in your updated house manual that has house rules and shows which items are off-limits. Put up notes like where they can hang wet towels, remind them to drain water after using an iron, and remind them to use provided trash cans for any waste.

▷ Information Guide

Whether you choose to add this on the house manual or a separate one is entirely up to you. Guests do appreciate having some things spelled out for them, like recommendations of nearby attractions. For instance, if there are yoga sessions at sunrise by the beach, game drives, bird watching, painting classes, or art exhibitions at a nearby gallery, have these as options that guests can do to unwind or to make their stay more memorable. You can also recommend your favorite restaurants, when happy hour takes place at a local bar, or whether there are any traditional celebrations that they may want to experience. Not only do guests appreciate these, but there is a sense of safety when opting for things you have recommended and can vouch for.

Another way to ensure that you meet your guests' needs is by availing yourself via text or on call for anything. If you will not be there for some time, you can include numbers for a handyman, security, cable support, go-to neighbor, or any emergency personnel that can come to their rescue should a need arise in your absence.

▷ Provide Entertainment

If your property does not have entertaining amenities like a pool or Jacuzzi, don't worry; think out of the box and provide other fun activities to do. You can include board games, books, Netflix, or Disney+ to ensure guests are not bored during their stay. Of course, you don't have to provide every channel or unlimited subscription as some people might take advantage of your generosity and exploit you. You can lock or set your remote, Netflix, or Disney+ accounts to have limited guest mode that only offers what you deem necessary. One superhost said that he includes new movies that he may have rented on his listings as well, and has received incredible reviews from guests (AirbnbUncovered, 2020). Remember that your goal is to make profit while making guests feel great, so don't go for expensive amenities if you cannot afford them.

Step #5: Work Towards a Great Review

The reason you should pay attention to how your guests feel in your home is because this industry is reliant on reviews. Your star rating is the lifeblood of your business, so ensure that you work towards getting a great review from guests. This is why I said with some things you have to go beyond your call of duty to be thoughtful for your guests and be more accommodating. Don't sweat the small stuff, but that does not mean you should be a walkover in the name of reviews. Maintain politeness at all times.

You will be reviewed on things like communication, cleanliness, and the precision of your location as opposed to what you mentioned in your listing, so be careful not to exaggerate that your property is a stone's throw from a particular attraction if it's beyond a handful of miles. You will also be reviewed on the whole experience, so ensure that you leave a warm memory for your guests and that your partnering third parties are in alignment with your service as mentioned in the mission statement.

Regardless of consistent five stars, one bad review can reduce your rating or even cost you your superhost status. That is why it is important to make sure that you provide the best hospitality you possibly can. Some things are not worth losing your cool over in front of your guest. For instance, if they accidentally break a glass, stain your rug with nail polish, and they are honest enough to let you know, don't show your irritation, but be more understanding of that little accident —even though you know it might cost you expensive stain remover or having to replace a broken item. In your rules you would have already included damage costs, and Airbnb does provide insurance for property damage (even though it does not cover everything). You can also send your guest a reminder to pay for damaged property, which they already know they have to cover as stipulated in the terms and conditions.

Airbnb reviews are two-way; you as a host also have to leave a review on the guest. Just as a positive review is important to your business, you have to be mindful of what you say about a guest as this will determine how other hosts will take their booking request in future. You don't want to ruin their chances just as you don't want them to leave a bad review on you. Airbnb has updated its review policy, whereby neither of you can see the other's review before you have left a review. It also allows you to leave a public review about the guest and also a private review that will only be visible to them—that's where I feel like you should address your dissatisfaction so they know that they need to work on themselves—without hurting their chances of being accepted in future.

Bear in mind that the review that you have left or have received determines the future relationship between you and your guest. You don't know what might cause them to return to your area and that can help your long-term relationship. They may even recommend your place to friends and family. It is paramount that you also take reviews seriously. Listen to what grievances they had about your place and use them to improve your establishment, rather than being offended.

KEY POINTS

- Attending to your guests' needs is the blueprint for success in this business.
- Aim to offer exceptional services and you will not only gain great reviews and more money, but you'd have opened a door of friendship.
- You don't have to break your budget to provide the best amenities; just be thoughtful, creative, and attentive to your guests' needs and you will gain raving fans and great reviews for your listing.

8

BECOMING A SUPERHOST

One way to raise the bar in the Airbnb business is to get the most sought after Superhost status. Becoming a superhost is more than acquiring the recognition badge to display on your profile, but it's the quickest way to make a killing with high earnings and consistent bookings.

THE SUPERHOST OVERVIEW

What Is a Superhost?

A superhost is an Airbnb recognized and revered host or property manager who goes above and beyond the call of duty to make their guests feel accommodated and appreciated. Becoming a superhost is not something that can be applied for, but Airbnb automatically grants this recognition to hosts that meet the required criteria by giving guests an outstanding experience. This status is earned in this industry and is what every host aspires to be and maintain for the exceptional privileges that come with it.

How Long Does it Take to Become a Superhost?

Climbing this ladder is not that hard or dependent on years of experience. You can be a new host and still qualify for the superhost badge before long as long as you meet the required selection criteria. Airbnb usually uses your 12 months' bookings to determine if you qualify for recognition, which it filters every three months to review any qualifying hosts. However, you don't have to wait a full year before you're awarded your status. If you match all requirements, the duration to work for this milestone is entirely up to you. You can take half a year, three months, or less, but your status will be awarded when Airbnb does its quarterly search.

Why Should You Become a Superhost?

The superhost recognition is one of the great perks that you definitely want to enjoy as a reward for the work you do, going an extra mile to ensure that your guests are satisfied. It is not just the badge that Airbnb attaches to your profile—there are several add-ons that come with this recognition as the benefits below elaborate.

▷ More Bookings

It's no secret that once you've acquired this badge, you've set yourself apart from the rest of the market and you have the competitive edge over other hosts in your area. This means that you're likely to have an increase in bookings as guests want to experience your magic and what has other guests raving about your place. The fear of missing out (FOMO) effect is what will get people wanting to check your place out so that they can also rave to their friends about how they stayed at this incredible place. This also means that, besides the reviews on the platform, guests will refer their friends and family to your place. You also come off as trustworthy to guests, which means that guests will likely book a recognized superhost because they trust that they have been vetted and thus appear as a safer option.

▷ More Money

This should be obvious from the influx of bookings coming as stated above, however there are more reasons to this. As a superhost, it's no secret that your amenities are better and your service is exceptional. This means that you can adjust your rates and people will still opt for your place over cheaper ones. You can get away with increasing your prices, thereby making more money per booking. People don't usually complain about superhosts being too expensive because they know they will get value for their money. So this flexibility with your rates allows you to throw in more perks and adjust rates as you see fit.

▷ Higher Visibility on the Platform

As a badged host, your listing gets priority whenever similar searches are conducted or any keywords that are on your details make your listing shown first. If a guest searches and your listing pops up first on the platform, that usually means your listing gets more clicks, which then increases your booking rate. Being a superhost gives you the perk of being trusted by many guests as the badge proves that you go above and beyond for your guests.

Another visibility opportunity is that you may get featured in the Airbnb listing, which is distributed to all subscribers. This means that you might get extra publicity. Moreover, you can be invited to local Airbnb events where you will network with other hosts and get industry recognition.

▷ Priority Support

All hosts are valuable members of Airbnb and thus receive support should they have any queries. However, as a superhost, you get priority support, which means an issue that could take days to resolve for an ordinary host will receive almost immediate attention. Some guests tend to take advantage of the refund policy that allows free stays when they can prove that the reception of a host was hostile or unclean. These chancers may win over ordinary hosts, but for superhosts, the Airbnb team puts this issue more under the microscope to establish what went wrong. When the issue gets resolved, it's usually in favor of the superhost.

▷ The Superhost Search Filter

When guests want to select their next rentals by narrowing their search for superhosts only, your listing also goes into that filtered search. Instead of the obvious elimination other hosts get, it gets prioritized.

▷ Bonus Referral Income

Superhosts get a 20% higher bonus on the referral program when inviting other hosts to the platform. This means that you may have referred the same number of hosts as an ordinary host, but your commission is 20% more than what the other gets even though you would have contributed the same effort.

▷ Travel Coupons

Some of the perks of being a superhost include a yearly $100 travel coupon given by Airbnb. If you maintain your status yearly, then you get that $100 coupon, which you can use to explore and stay at other places to explore, do research, or simply for pleasure travel.

The Superhost Criteria

What does it actually take for a host to be given such a prestigious recognition of superhost status? What do you need to do to qualify? Great questions! I used to think that this was a far-fetched dream until I realized how easy it was to fit the requirements for this sought-after status. The major key is that Airbnb monitors the performance of every host on their platform, rewards those that deserve recognition, and strips off the benefits to those that do not measure up.

▷ Host 10 Guests or More in One Year

Airbnb requires at least ten fulfilled reservations within a period of 12 months or three reservations that total at least 100 nights each for one to be considered for the superhost status. The good news is that there doesn't have to be consecutive bookings as long as they fit within the specified period. You have to agree that, regardless of where your property is located or how highly competitive your area is, 10 reservations in a year is pretty easy. During peak season, achieving this milestone is a walk in the park, while during off-peak it might take a lot of effort to bag those bookings. At the increasing rate of travelers post-extreme COVID-19 lockdown restrictions, any host can easily tick off this requirement and focus on the next point.

It is important to note that even though Airbnb judges you based on 12 months of hosting, you can be granted superhost status as soon as you meet the requirements, even if it has not been a year. This means that you can climb this recognition ladder even if you're fairly new into this industry, as long as you tick all of the boxes.

▷ Maintain a 90% Response Rate

This is where it gets interesting. The communication that we've emphasized throughout the book is a crucial factor towards superhost qualification. Airbnb requires that no guest should wait long for a response. Not all guests are patient; if they have sent a request and the host takes long to respond, they move on to the next one. For hosts that go above and beyond to respond promptly at a 90% rate or higher to all guest messages, Airbnb rewards this as good service and it's another check used to grant superhost status.

▷ Have One Percent or Lower Cancellation Rate

Unless under unavoidable circumstances, Airbnb requires that you keep guest reservation cancellations at the lowest possible minimum. This means that in 100 guests, you should not cancel more than one booking. You don't want to cause a situation where a guest is frustrated with your last minute cancellation that requires them to settle for unsatisfactory accommodation because you disappointed them.

▷ Maintain a 4.8 and Above Rating

When it comes to reviews and overall rating, you need to strive for a near perfect score. Anything less than 4.8 is average, and that is not superhost standard. You'll get the best rating when your guests are satisfied with your service. Strive to get a high score on all aspects like communication, cleanliness, location accuracy, and hospitality. The more reviews you have, the better your chances of having a once in a while guest with a negative review affecting or reducing your score.

Tips to Becoming a Superhost

▷ Quality Photos

Photos are generally the first thing that sells your property online. In a highly competitive industry such as this, you will find your listing compared to many others, and you want to make sure that it stands out. Great, professionally taken photos of your property will give you a competitive edge amongst the best listings. It is advisable that you take this exercise seriously and invest in having quality photos displaying your property. Many hosts add many photos in the reel that show similar angles and not much focus on the amenities of the property. This is a futile exercise as what matters is the quality of photos with different angles that highlight the best amenities of the property.

▷ Communicate Effectively

To maintain a 90% response rate, you either have to be full-time employed by your business to answer messages all day long or hire an assistant who's dedicated to managing your calendar and responding to messages. These two options are doable but prone to cause problems when you and your assistant are held up with another guest and there are incoming messages that need your attention. While some superhosts with a manageable number of properties say that they prefer real human interaction instead of full-on automated messages, the industry has evolved and continues to grow to the extent whereby 30% of listings on a particular area can be properties managed by one person (Robuilt, 2022). This enormous growth leads to a need to have autoresponders embedded for effective communication.

▷ Automate Your Home

As it stands, to become a superhost means that you have to handle an influx of short-term or long-term bookings, hence more money. But it also means a lot more responsibility. You cannot just rely on automated messages and think that once you keep up with the 90% communication rate your job gets easier. You need to automate everything that is scalable to maintain uniformity of efficiency throughout your entire hospitality. This means that you need to use property management services, automate cleaning communication, restock your supplies, and seek tech help in order to maintain an exceptional track record without any physical or mental burnout. From smart locks to autoresponders, there are many host assist applications that you can use today to make your job easier and make money while having freedom to do other things important to you.

You need systems in place for you to maintain a level of efficiency so that this also does not become a burden to you. Joe Gebbia says one of the pieces of advice given to them during the early stages of setting up the Airbnb marketplace was to find a way to scale, bearing in mind that not everything is scalable (Greylock, 2015). Some duties need a personal touch, so save your energy for these kinds of activities that demand your active involvement and leave the rest to automation. You don't have to hand-in the keys to every new guest if you have smart locks, nor do you have to call the cleaning services after the guest checks out, if you have systems that can detect a series of events and roll out on their own.

▷ Don't Cancel Unless You Have To

We've already mentioned that you can only qualify for this status if you have one percent or less cancellation rate, so you need to keep it that way. This can be rather difficult if you have listed your property on a number of different marketplaces as you can be double-booked and have to cancel another guest who is already looking forward to staying at your home. Canceling a guest's booking not only makes them feel rejected, but it also highly inconveniences their plans, which all leave a bitter taste and bad feelings towards your property. While you are not likely to encounter the issue of double bookings if your property is only listed on Airbnb as it syncs your calendar, some superhosts advise listing your property on other marketplaces so that your occupancy rate is maximized.

▷ **Make Sure Your Guests Leave Reviews**

Remember that reviews are earned, so go out of your way to ensure that you deliver exceptional service that leaves a guest no choice but to commend you. It's everything you do from when a client books your place, arrives, and the entire experience until they leave your property that contributes towards positive reviews. You can even go as far as letting them know that you would appreciate a positive review as reviews help you stay in business. There's nothing wrong with a blunt request like that. Bear in mind that you have to maintain a 4.8 or above review rating.

KEY POINTS

- You can achieve an esteemed Airbnb superhost status even if you are new in this business.
- Achieve this by improving your communication, not canceling your bookings, maintaining a great review score, and going above and beyond to improve your guest's experience.

Now, you can put all your newfound information to good use! For the next and final chapter, you will gain some practical tips and tricks to succeed in your Airbnb business.

9

THE FINAL AIRBNB TIPS

With incredible testimonies on social media of successful hosts like Michael Elefante, whose properties brought in a revenue of $65,000 in one month, an Airbnb business model is a lucrative way to make loads of money from vacation rentals (Medina, 2021). As we've already dissected, it doesn't matter how small you start, whether it's a one bedroom in a rented apartment where you are also staying or it's a set of curated luxury apartments across different tourist drawing locations; you can benefit from this easy to manage business model. Depending on your goals, Airbnb is a willing and fueled vehicle to take you to your destination in the hospitality and real estate industry. In this chapter, we'll go through some of the best tips from successful Airbnb superhosts. Following some of these tips that have proven to be a success routine, find the ones that can fit in with your unit or incorporate the ones that you've been lenient on so that you can smile from getting the best out of this investment.

Tip #1: Be Honest and Truthful

This business is designed for trust, coexistence, economy sharing, and relationship building. It relies on honesty and the truth. The best way to avoid any bad reviews and maintain the great standards of Airbnb, remember to always operate with full disclosure of the condition of your property, the rules that apply, and what your expectations are. You also have to be honest enough when giving reviews so that you always receive honest reviews. There's no need to oversell your property, because that can lead to high expectations which would be followed by huge disappointments and terrible reviews. Ensure that there are no illusioned images that may give the guest the wrong idea about your property. You don't want to come off as an untrustworthy host with shady operations, because reputation is everything in this business. Protect yours by running your business as honestly and as truthful as possible.

Tip #2: Make Sure Your Rules Are Clear and Concise

When starting a new business, especially in a niche that one is not an expert in, it's easy to tolerate a lot of ill-treatment in the name of being more accommodative. Be careful not to have your kindness and humanity exploited by being too understanding to a point that you don't call out bad behavior. Make your rules clear and easy to understand. Reiterate that guests should treat your home with respect just as they would their homes. If you don't want parties thrown at your place, be clear about it and stipulate that there will be a fine should rules be violated. If your property is a non-smoking zone, does not allow pets, or any rules that apply to your establishment, be concise about them so that guests know what they are walking into and they have no reason to call you a liar while leaving a bad review about what a control freak you are. It's your property at the end of the day, and if you want to please everyone, there will be a high price to pay through damages, relationships with your neighbors, or even terrible reviews that can lead you to being banned from the platform.

Tip #3: Make Sure You Have Enough Time Between Bookings

Manage your calendar in such a way that it gives you allowance to prepare for the next booking. Nothing turns off guests like walking into the previous guest's residual waste. While it's tempting to have consecutive bookings, depending on the size of your unit and efficiency of your cleaning team, make allowance to have enough time to ensure that the place is spotless, supplies are restocked, and the unit looks and smells fresh and ready for the next guest. There might be unforeseen circumstances that may require the leaving guest to stay a bit longer, or need to leave their stuff behind for a while after checkout, or there might be an emergency that requires an incoming guest to have to check-in earlier. You don't want to have to find yourself favoring the other more while dismissing the other. as they are both important for your business. Allow at least a day in between to have enough time to prepare. Another way you can be able to get away with consecutive bookings is having extra amenities and supplies nearby for easy changing of linen and restocked supplies.

Tip #4: Take Advantage of Airbnb Customer Service if You Have Any Issues

Use the provided resources by Airbnb to solve difficult guests or in the event that there are disputes. Airbnb is designed to protect both the guest and the host, so if there are any issues that seem tricky to handle in person, contact support and be assisted. File a complaint if a guest has left your property in an unsatisfactory manner (serious damage) and the customer service agent will go through the issue with you to find a resolution. They might ask the client to cover the damages if they want to continue using the platform or they can use the allocated funds for such incidents.

Tip #5: Pay Attention to Details, Guests Love It

We've already reiterated what it takes to become a superhost: You need to go an extra mile to accommodate your guest. Pay attention to detail and pick up drops of hints from your conversation to incorporate in your planned treats or anything to make their experience memorable. For instance, if the guest hinted their reason for the trip in your area during early communication, be sure to note it and suggest things that could either enhance that experience or try to incorporate that into the welcome gift theme. This will show that you were attentive of them and went above and beyond for them to have a great time.

Tip #6: Consider Allowing Instant Bookings

If you have not yet automated your communication, it may take time to get around responding to all messages, queries, and booking requests. Some guests are not patient with delayed service and you might end up losing that guest as they're likely to move on to a more responsive host. Consider allowing instant bookings, trusting that Airbnb will automatically accept that booking, and later you can do your vetting after the guest has already been booked. This is bound to raise your bookings and increase your response rate. Just make sure that you've listed all rules pertaining to your house so that you have a leg to stand on should there be any misunderstandings.

Tip #7: Make Sure You Understand the Cancellation Policies

Whether it's due to extenuating circumstances or minor differences between guests and hosts, there are up to three cancellation policies that Airbnb uses. In the event that a booking is canceled seven days prior to check-in, up to 50% of the booking fee can be refunded. The service fee that goes to Airbnb is refundable if a cancellation is made within 48 hours of booking, up to three times a year. The cleaning fees are fully refunded if the guest decides to cancel their reservation. However, if the guest cancels in less than seven days before local check-in time or they decide to leave earlier than their intended stay, the nights booked cannot be refunded (Mar, 2020).

In the case that there are extenuating circumstances that require the host to cancel, the guest will be refunded, but for any disputes, the guest and the host can liaise with Airbnb within 24 hours of check-in. Whatever Airbnb deems necessary, it has the power to give final decisions on all disputes. You need to be aware and fully understand these policies so that you're protected from any manipulation and you are saved from losses.

Tip #8: Strive For Superhost Status

The ultimate goal of any Airbnb host is to become a recognized superhost. Considering advantages like being able to set your own price, receiving yearly travel coupons, and more bookings amongst other things, you need to strive to achieve the superhost status and maintain it. Aim to have more guests wowed by your exceptional service to provoke them to leave those great reviews.

Tip #9: Always Do More Than You Promised

In relation to the point above, you will have an upper hand over your clients and other hosts when you always do more than you promised. Aim to overdeliver on your promises, service, and hospitality, then you will have great reviews, more money, and exponential growth in your business. You'll also feel great knowing that you made your guests feel great. Most superhosts confessed that going above and beyond for their guests have earned them great reviews, return guests, and they have even had their acts of kindness and generosity reciprocated (Daly, 2021).

Tip #10: Send Guests Reminders

It's possible that some guests might have made bookings some time ago and the important information like your basic rules, directions, what to do when checking in, or anything worth noting might be long forgotten. It won't hurt to send them a reminder in their email the night before check-in so that they remember what to expect regarding your property.

Tip #11: Leave Explanations Around the House for Your Guests

Even with the house manual and a set of instructions briefly explaining how everything works, it's possible to make mistakes. Leave notes around the house showing how your appliances work, reminding them to hang wet towels, which switch is for which bulb, and where paper waste goes. This way, not only do you make navigating your house less frustrating for someone who isn't used to how everything operates, you also save yourself the trouble of having to fix your appliances which are misused and being contacted and asked about the tiniest details that guests can get around to without your involvement.

Tip #12: Never Underestimate the Power of Decoration

There's something about walking into a well-decorated house. First, it shows off your artistic style, unique taste, and attention to detail; it also shows that you made an effort to make the house homey, and it's a way of letting the guest into your life or anything that interests you. A decorated house refreshes the look of the entire house, making it a welcoming space for the guest to work or feel more at home. Decoration also makes your listing photos standout and prompt clicks. People are drawn to beautiful spaces with an interesting tale to tell. Depending on the size of your property, you can either go for the minimalist theme with natural colors, be playful and contrast colors if you want, or share paintings and souvenirs from across the world so that your decor leaves a fond memory to a guest about your place.

You can also be intentional about making your space beautiful by hiring a professional interior designer to revamp the entire house. Your bedding, rugs, and furniture can tell an interesting and artistic story that guests will cherish.

Tip #13: Avoid Taking Bookings Outside of Airbnb

As much as I've shared that you can list your property on different platforms and that you can own your clients by collecting their emails, avoid taking bookings outside of the Airbnb platform as that may lead to problems. You lose protection or cover of damage as well as support when you've taken a booking privately; Airbnb is unable to settle the issue that occurred outside of its platform. It also helps you to have your own insurance as Airbnb does not cover everything.

Tip #14: Automate Your Business

Even if you love hosting, you don't want to be fully employed by your business. Make things easier for yourself by automating communication, using property management services, and use smart locks to avoid loss of keys and to make check-in super easy. You want the business that requires less from you, as that's where financial freedom is derived: making money passively or with less effort. Use available tools to have your autoresponders set, have cleaners contacted automatically upon guest checkout, and anything you can incorporate to make your life easier so that you can focus on expanding your business.

KEY POINTS

- Honesty is the best policy when it comes to your listing; it will help you avoid setting too high expectations that fall flat and lead to negative reviews.
- Pay attention to detail and go above and beyond to leave a fond and positive memory for your

guests. Decoration goes a long way to show that you made an effort with your place.

- Strive for the superhost badge and enjoy the benefits that come with this status.
- Understand cancellation policies and take advantage of Airbnb customer care services to settle any disputes.
- Automation will save you time and make you more money, so consider automating your business.

There you have it, all the information you need to become another thriving Airbnb investor. Cheers to your successful journey!

LEAVE A 1-CLICK REVIEW

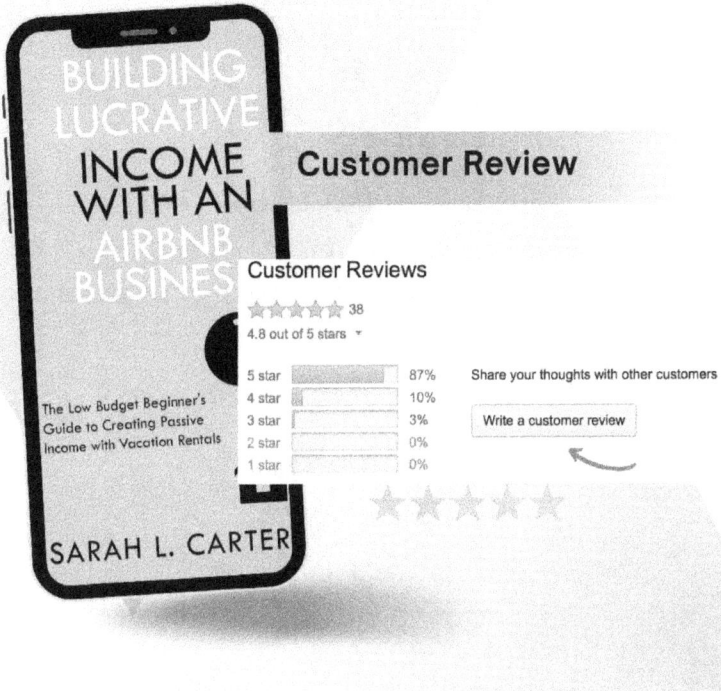

I would be incredibly thankful if you could take **60** seconds to write a belief review on Amazon, even if it is just a few sentences.

It will not only help me but many along the way.

Scan the QR code below to leave your review.

You can also join my Facebook group by scanning the QR code below.

CONCLUSION

With all that has been expressed in this comprehensive guide to low budget methods of creating passive income through vacation rentals, I have no doubt that you are resourceful and ready to kick off your plan into action. As already discussed, Airbnb is still in its infancy phase, even though it's over 15 years in operation. With its wide selection of properties that hosts list, it is kept trendy as people think out of the box to repurpose their available space. It also allows both the guests and hosts to experiment with untapped potential to keep things exciting and thrilling.

You can start your Airbnb from the limited resources you already have at your disposal and grow it into a massive profit-generating business that affords you the best of life. Acquiring and reading this book is one of the greatest decisions you made. While this book cannot contain everything you need to succeed in this business, I hope that it has given you the basic information and pointed to further resources that you can use to build massive wealth with the rental business.

To bring it further home, let's recap on the key points shared in this book. Market research will save you a lot of trouble and give you an upper hand to design a unique approach that will set you apart from the rest. Go into this business with the aim for success, which means you have to be ready to go above and beyond to provide exceptional service and give guests an exhilarating experience; your growth will be a given. It's important to remember that in the hospitality business, first impressions and the overall energy people draw from you last longest. Moreover, this business relies on reviews, so work for them if you want to mark your territory as a badged superhost. Your success depends on you offering quality service and leaving people better than before they met you.

Just with every phenomenal success story shared in this book, you are a wonder waiting to happen. Against all odds, the founders of Airbnb built this company from the ground up, with its success causing a ripple effect by changing millions of people's lives. Find your starting point and go for it! You have nothing to be wary of. If I could go from living on one paycheck that barely met my minimum needs to having multiple streams of income through Airbnb, surely I'm a living testimony and in a position to tell you that you can do it. Grab the baton from me and run into your own success story using the right tools provided within. If you've been impacted by this book, kindly leave a review so that someone's life can also be changed!

REFERENCES

8 Not-so-obvious ways to promote your Airbnb listing. (2018, July 26). IGMS. https://www.igms.com/promote-your-airbnb-listing/

9NEWS. (2019, June 12). *Couple accused of illegally running short-term rental business through Airbnb.* YouTube [Video] https://www.youtube.com/watch?v=31xilDor_3g

10 Airbnb tools that all hosts need to maximize income. (2019, June 24). Whome. https://whome.pt/blog/airbnb-tools

Abulatif, N. (2019, March 21). *What Airbnb investors need to know before buying rental properties.* Investment Prop-

erty Tips | Mashvisor Real Estate Blog. https://www.
mashvisor.com/blog/airbnb-investors-buying-
properties/

Airbnb. (2017, April 11). *Tips for hosting guests long-term.*
The Airbnb Blog - Belong Anywhere. https://blog.
atairbnb.com/long-term-stays

Airbnb. (2019a, July 19). *Making a hosting business plan -
Resource Center.* Airbnb. https://www.airbnb.co.za/
resources/hosting-homes/a/making-a-hosting-busi
ness-plan-98?locale=en&_set_bev_on_new_domain=
1651173858_NmVlMzY0MWM5YmQx

Airbnb. (2019b, November 20). *How to welcome your first
guests - Resource Center.* Airbnb. https://www.airbnb.co.
za/resources/hosting-homes/a/how-to-welcome-
your-first-guests-32?locale=en&_set_bev_on_new_do
main=1651173858_NmVlMzY0MWM5YmQx

Airbnb. (2020a, June 10). *Elevate the guest experience with
these tips from the pros - Resource Center* Airbnb. https://
www.airbnb.co.za/resources/hosting-homes/a/
elevate-the-guest-experience-with-these-tips-from-
the-pros-239?locale=en&_set_bev_on_new_domain=
1651173858_NmVlMzY0MWM5YmQx

Airbnb. (2020b, July 10). *Airbnb: Vacation rentals, cabins, beach houses, unique homes & experiences.* Airbnb. https://www.airbnb.com/resources/hosting-homes/a/elevate-the-guest-experien

Airbnb. (2020c, November 19). *Airbnb: Vacation rentals, cabins, beach houses, Unique homes & experiences.* Airbnb. https://www.airbnb.com/resources/hosting-homes/a/the-amenities-guests-wan

Airbnb 101. (2020, April 21). *The 3 main Airbnb host categories: Which one are you?* BnB Hosts. https://www.bnbhosts.com.au/3-airbnb-host-categories/

Airbnb Automated. (2018, March 19). *Airbnb cohosting walkthrough | How to be or train a co-host for your short term rental business.* YouTube [Video] https://www.youtube.com/watch?v=XJXr_sIBfdg

Airbnb Automated. (2019a, July 23). *3 Guaranteed ways to get more bookings.* YouTube [Video] https://www.youtube.com/watch?v=vuk6j_gWtVs

Airbnb Automated. (2019b, December 24). *My 5 biggest mistakes growing an Airbnb business.* YouTube [Video] https://www.youtube.com/watch?v=OeenLS7krWg

Airbnb Automated. (2020, October 14). *MUST HAVE Amenities for your vacation rental in 2021.* YouTube [Video] https://www.youtube.com/watch?v=WwsMIChMDfE

Airbnb Automated. (2022a, January 28). *HOW TO START AN AIRBNB BUSINESS STEP BY STEP IN 2022.* YouTube [Video] https://www.youtube.com/watch?v=RANqKCKK6QE

Airbnb Automated. (2022b, February 1). *Real Airbnb pros and cons 2022 should you start an Airbnb business or is it too late?* YouTube [Video] https://www.youtube.com/watch?v=pXAiZlwcALY

Airbnb furnishing tips and tricks - Rentingyourplace.com. (n.d.). Renting Your Place. http://rentingyourplace.com/airbnb-101/furnishing

Airbnb statistics and host insights [2022]. (2022, February). The Zebra. https://www.thezebra.com/resources/home/airbnb-statistics

Airbnb Titles: Proven Formulas That Attract 5x More Bookings. (2020, April 27). IGMS. https://www.igms.com/airbnb-titles/

AirbnbUncovered. (2020). *Airbnb hosting amenities - Which leave guests raving?* YouTube [Video] https://www.youtube.com/watch?v=K-ebSNA58Pk

AirDNA | How our data works. (n.d.). AirDNA. https://www.airdna.co/airdna-data-how-it-works

Alcaniz, R. (2021). *Airbnb vs Booking.com – Where is it better to host your property?* YouTube [Video] https://www.youtube.com/watch?v=iULlWZ9YfAw

Ambrosio, D. (2018, June 16). *The six types of Airbnb hosts.* Creative Roam. https://creativeroam.com/blog/the-six-types-of-airbnb-hosts/

Amer. (2021, February 2). *My experience with furnished finder as a landlord.* YouTube [Video] https://www.youtube.com/watch?v=dZaxmQoY3a8

Andrew, K. (2020, March 16). *Best rental tax deductions for vacation and Airbnb business (How to pay zero taxes).* YouTube [Video] https://www.youtube.com/watch?v=nQEP_uu34dA

Andrew, K. (2021, May 11). *Knowing the basics of all zoning laws.* YouTube [Video] https://www.youtube.com/watch?v=g43qIgsZdeY

ARAJ, V. (2022, March 31). *Buying an investment property: Everything you need to know* Rocket Mortgage https://www.rocketmortgage.com/learn/investment-property

Arroyo, A. (2020a, November 24). *HOW I CREATED 6 FIGURES in Airbnb revenue in 1 YEAR- Starting your own short term rental business.* YouTube [Video] https://www.youtube.com/watch?v=QRZv6iMR2JA

Arroyo, A. (2020b, November 26). *HOW TO BECOME A 5 STAR AIRBNB SUPERHOST.* YouTube [Video] https://www.youtube.com/watch?v=V6uqkIxDKEA

As Within Algenay. (2021, September 25). *Why I'm quitting my Airbnb business with receipts | How much I made | Pros & Cons #airbnb.* YouTube [Video] https://www.youtube.com/watch?v=PoJzvwn_mRc

Baker, G. (2020, October 5). *115 Real estate words to spice up your property listings.* Fit Small Business. https://fitsmallbusiness.com/real-estate-words/

Becker, S. (2020, January 22). *How this 37-year-old makes $34,000 per year in extra income—as an Airbnb host.* CNBC. https://www.cnbc.com/2020/01/22/how-this-millennial-makes-34000-a-year-in-extra-incomeas-an-airbnb-host.html

Bermudiana Beach Resort. (2020, May 7). *The pros & cons of Airbnb that owners need to know*. Bermudiana https://www.bermudiana.com/blog/the-pros-cons-of-airbnb-that-owners-need-to-know

BnB Hosts Team. (2020, April 21). *The 3 main Airbnb host categories: Which one are you?* BnB Hosts. https://www.bnbhosts.com.au/3-airbnb-host-categories/

Cardone, G. (2019, July 3). *How to generate wealth with Air BNB - Ask the pro with Grant Cardone & Brian Page*. YouTube [Video] https://www.youtube.com/watch?v=J0H6l1wjmd8

Cassie Villela, Realtor - Silverbridge Realty. (2021, June 30). *Review: Furnished Finder*. YouTube [Video] https://www.youtube.com/watch?v=BT-grKMDiIY

Chaffey, D. (2020, August 3). *Global social media research summary August 2020 | Smart Insights*. Smart Insights. https://www.smartinsights.com/social-media-marketing/social-media-strategy/new-global-social-media-research

Chamberlain, J. (2021, June 9). *Airbnb taxes | Tax tips for short-term rental owners | Vacation homes*. Gunn Chamberlain. https://www.gunnchamberlain.com/tax-tips-short-term-rentals-airbnb-taxes-v

Craig, A. (2017, November). *Andrew Craig's recent interview with the CEO of Furnished Finder*. Furnished Finder. https://www.furnishedfinder.com/blog/Andrew-Craig-interview

Curry, D. (2020, August 25). *Airbnb Revenue and usage statistics (2020)*. Business of Apps. https://www.businessofapps.com/data/airbnb-statistics/

Daly, A. (2021, March 13). *25 Insanely useful Airbnb tips that will make you a better host*. BuzzFeed. https://www.buzzfeed.com/anniedaly/pro-tips-from-airbnb-superhosts

DiLallo, M. (2022, April 12). *How to invest in real estate*. The Motley Fool. https://www.fool.com/investing/stock-market/market-sectors/real-estate-investing/

Dixon, A. (2018, May 21). *Top 10 components of a good business plan*. SmartAsset; SmartAsset. https://smartasset.com/small-business/top-components-of-a-business-plan

EHL Insights. (n.d.). *Why do people stay in Airbnb?* Hospitality Insights https://hospitalityinsights.ehl.edu/travel ers-airbnb-study

Elefante, M. (2020, December 9). *How much it COSTS to operate an Airbnb - The TRUTH.* YouTube [Video] https://www.youtube.com/watch?v=LXqlRu2lqdc

Everything you need to know about how Airbnb works for hosts. (2018, July 17). Q4Launch. https://q4launch.com/blog/how-airbnb-works-for-hysts/

Folger, J. (2021, December 23). *How Airbnb works.* Investopedia. https://www.investopedia.com/articles/personal-finance/032814/pros-and-cons-using-airbn

Fortune Magazine. (2017). Interview with Airbnb CEO Brian Chesky | Fortune [YouTube Video]. https://www.youtube.com/watch?v=GFMeuSIhIYg

Fundersandfounders. (2014, June 27). *How AirBnB started - Founding story.* YouTube [Video] https://www.youtube.com/watch?v=axqh6SJOO0c

Greylock. (2015). Airbnb's Joe Gebbia: "Do things that don't scale" YouTube [Video] https://www.youtube.com/watch?v=2hESOWxPrSU

Griffiths, C. (2020, February 19). *How to conduct an Airbnb market analysis | Expert advice.* Lifty Life. https://www.liftylife.ca/airbnb-market-analysis/

Grothaus, M. (2015, March 26). *How to make a killing on Airbnb.* Fast Company. https://www.fastcompany.com/3043468/the-secrets-of-airbnb-superhosts

Host requirements - Airbnb Help Center. (n.d.). Airbnb. https://www.airbnb.co.za/help/article/576/host-requirements

Hosthub. (2018, March 7). *What is Hosthub (formerly Syncbnb)?* YouTube [Video] https://www.youtube.com/watch?v=sS36ngK60qA

Hosting team permissions - Airbnb Help Center. (n.d.). Airbnb. Retrieved May 10, 2022, from https://www.airbnb.co.za/help/article/2513/hosting-team-permissions

How Much? (2019, April 9). *How much can you make on Airbnb - Superhost revenue.* YouTube [Video] https://www.youtube.com/watch?v=_JUCDgm8140

How to make your Airbnb family friendly. (2018, April 23).

Guest Ready. https://www.guestready.com/blog/airbnb-family-friendly/

Iacob, R. (2019). *The Best Software For Airbnb Rental Market Analysis | AirDNA.* YouTube [Video] https://www.youtube.com/watch?v=Y0WnxLpurkw

iGMS. (2016, December 15). *7 Airbnb SEO Tips for Airbnb Entrepreneur.* IGMS. https://www.igms.com/airbnb-seo/

iGMS. (2019a, November 13). *Airbnb marketing strategy: 6 techniques to crush your competitors.* IGMS. https://www.igms.com/airbnb-marketing-strategy/

iGMS. (2019b, November 27). *Airbnb rules: 6-step checklist to stay within the law.* IGMS. https://www.igms.com/airbnb-rules/

IRS. (2018). *Forms & instructions | Internal Revenue Service.* IRS. https://www.irs.gov/forms-instructions

Jaber, D. (2018, February 20). *How to find a real estate agent for buying the best investment properties.* Investment Property Tips | Mashvisor Real Estate Blog. https://www.mashvisor.com/blog/find-a-real-estate-agent-buying-best-investment-properties/

Jaleesa, J. (2018, February 5). *Airbnb Statistics [2020]: User & Market Growth Data.* IPropertyManagement https://ipropertymanagement.com/research/airbnb-statistics

Jasper. (2019a, August 9). *Airbnb founder story: From selling cereals to a $25B company.* Get Paid for Your Pad. https://getpaidforyourpad.com/blog/the-airbnb-founder-story/

Jasper. (2019b, September 13). *Everything you need to know about scaling your Airbnb business.* Get Paid for Your Pad. https://getpaidforyourpad.com/blog/scaling-your-airbnb-business-guide/

Jasper. (2019c, September 30). *How to have an insanely good Airbnb photo section.* Get Paid for Your Pad. https://getpaidforyourpad.com/blog/ultimate-guide-creating-best-photo-section-airbnb-listing/

Jasper. (2020, April 17). *Writing an Airbnb bio that soothes potential guests during the pandemic.* Get Paid for Your Pad. https://getpaidforyourpad.com/blog/how-to-create-a-great-airbnb-profile/

Jose The ModernXer. (2021, November 6). *Is having an AirBnb rental worth it?* YouTube [Video] https://www.youtube.com/watch?v=8xsF2ygF4mM

Karani, A. (2020, May 10). *4 key Airbnb investment metrics you should know.* Investment Property Tips | Mashvisor Real Estate Blog. https://www.mashvisor. com/blog/airbnb-investment-metrics/#:~:text

Kaushik, S. (2021, September 12). *Rental arbitrage South Africa.* Airbtics | Airbnb Analytics. https://airbtics.com/ rental-arbitrage-south-africa

Kierra Castle. (2022, March). *WHY EVERYONE IS QUITTING AIRBNB #YOUREHOME.* YouTube [Video] https://www.youtube.com/watch?v=jAGMta-SkUg

Kiyosaki, R. (2022, February 1). *7 proven strategies for real estate investing.* Rich Dad. https://www.richdad. com/7-proven-strategies-real-estate-investing

Knowledge at Wharton Staff. (2017, April 26). *The inside story behind the unlikely rise of Airbnb.* Knowl-edge@Wharton. https://knowledge.wharton.upenn. edu/article/the-inside-story-behind-the-unlikely-rise-of-airbnb/

Lattice. (2017, October 30). *How defining values and culture helped Airbnb achieve worldwide success.* Resources for Humans. https://medium.com/ resources-for-humans/how-defining-values-and-culture-helped-airbnb-achieve-worldwide-success-ff7adef06092

LearnAirbnb. (2016). *Airbnb taxes and tax reporting tips.* YouTube [Video] https://www.youtube.com/watch?v=lbTqOwD_bLM

Lemke, T. (2022, January 6). *Pros and cons of Airbnb as an investment strategy.* The Balance. https://www.thebalance.com/pros-and-cons-of-airbnb-asan- investment-strategy-4776231

Lieber, R. (2015, August 14). Airbnb horror story points to need for precautions. *The New York Times.* https://www.nytimes.com/2015/08/15/your-money/airbnb-horror-story-points-to-need-for-precautions.html

Love and London. (2016). *How does Airbnb work? Airbnb 101 guide* [YouTube Video]. https://www.youtube.com/watch?v=XDdIenqWknI

Mar. (2020, June 29). *Great Airbnb tips for hosts from a long time Airbnb Super Host.* Once in a Lifetime Journey. https://www.onceinalifetimejourney.com/our-travel-tips-and-tricks/tips-for-airbnb-hosts/

Mashvisor. (2022, January 3). *How to analyze an Airbnb*

rental market like a professional investor. YouTube [Video] https://www.youtube.com/watch?v=PrmPnq0Xkyo

MBA Online | See Why AirBnb is so successful. (2018, July 20). Online Business UMD. https://onlinebusiness. umd.edu/blog/the-4-reasons-why-airbnb-is-so-successful/

McInnis, R. (2020, January 24). *AirBnB taxes: Everything you need to know for 2020 tax season.* Picnic's Blog! https://www.picnictax.com/blog/airbnb-tax-guide/#: ~:text=You%20do%20no

Medina, D. (2021, July 9). *What can you make investing in Airbnb properties? One Nashville host said he made over $65K in June.* Tennessean. https://eu.tennessean.com/ story/money/real-estate/2021/07/09/nashville-airbnb-invest-properties-how-much-revenue/ 7917945002/

Mohajer, T. (2019, November 6). *Council post: The power of a first impression and what makes a great homepage.* Forbes. https://www.forbes.com/sites/forbesagency council/2019/11/06/the-power-of-a-first-impression-and-what-makes-a-great-homepage/?sh= 1e42690168f0

Moodley, C. (2021, November 6). *Another beloved Cape Town hotel closes its doors*. www.iol.co.za. https://www.iol.co.za/travel/south-africa/western-cape/another-beloved-cape-town-hotel-closes-its-doors-00086060-c225-43bd-ab6e-0b9a67c3fc05

Mthethwa, C. (2021, March 26). *Mother City's Townhouse Hotel to shut doors after 50 years due to Covid-19 lockdown*. News24. https://www.news24.com/news24/southafrica/news/mother-citys-townhouse-hotel-to-shut-doors-after-50-years-due-to-covid-19-lockdown-20210326

No-Nonsense Airbnb. (2020, April 23). *What is Airbnb co-hosting? | What can co-hosts do | How do they get paid*. YouTube [Video] https://www.youtube.com/watch?v=RWIzZx9UDYA

No-Nonsense Airbnb. (2021a). *How to sync Airbnb calendar with Booking.com | Hosting quick tips*. YouTube [Video] https://www.youtube.com/watch?v=mMC1n2wC__s

No-Nonsense Airbnb. (2021b, May 23). *Airbnb vs VRBO - [15 key differences] All you need to know as a host*. YouTube [Video] https://www.youtube.com/watch?v=XAoyGjFtjow

Peerspace. (2022, April 25). Peerspace https://www.peer space.com/legal/terms/community-guidelines

Peter McKenzie Quotes. (n.d.). QuoteHD. http://www. quotehd.com/quotes/peter-mckenzie-quote-you-want-someone-who-is-reliable-trustworthy-and

Pimentel, G. (2021). *Airbnb vs Furnished Rentals | What business model works best for rental arbitrage?* YouTube [Video] https://www.youtube.com/watch?v= NDK8O_pHiZw

Primary Hosts: An introduction - Airbnb Help Center. (n.d.). Airbnb. https://www.airbnb.co.za/help/article/1536/ primary-hosts-an-introduction?locale=en& _set_bev_on_new_domain= 1651173858_NmVlMzY0MWM5YmQx

Rayner, T. (2021, March 15). *What is Airbnb and how does it work?* Android Authority. https://www.androidau thority.com/what-is-airbnb-and-how-it-works-951512/

Rhodes, J. (2019, January 31). *The worst hotel chains for complaints revealed.* Which? https://www.which.co.uk/ news/article/the-worst-hotel-chains-for-complaints-revealed-aNkVZ8o2Eew4

Robuilt. (2021, December 21). *THESE things will make you more money on Airbnb.* YouTube [Video] https://www.youtube.com/watch?v=w-HyF1wyMX0

Robuilt. (2022, February 22). *THIS is how you self-manage an Airbnb and why I'll never pay for a property manager.* YouTube [Video] https://www.youtube.com/watch?v=yImPrb-M1KE

Rohde, J. (2021, September 27). *House hacking: 5 key strategies to be successful.* Learn Roofstock. https://learn.roofstock.com/blog/house-hacking

Russell, J. (2015, August 26). *Airbnb removes top host in Asia from its service with no explanation.* TechCrunch. https://techcrunch.com/2015/08/26/airbnb-removes-top-host-in-asia-from-its-service-with-no-explanation/

Santoro, J. (2022, January 7). *Should you invest in Airbnb in 2022?* The Motley Fool. https://www.fool.com/investing/2022/01/07/should-you-invest-in-airbnb-in-2022/

Sarah, K. (2021, March 14). *How we made $10,000 in our first month of being airbnb hosts.* Adventurous Couples and Family Travel Blog. https://hopscotchtheglobe. com/airbnb-host-success-story/

Short Term Sage - Airbnb, Vacation Rental Host. (2019, November 11). *What to put in your Airbnb listing description and title.* YouTube [Video] https://www.youtube. com/watch?v=porL7SKTpDA

Short Term Sage - Airbnb, Vacation Rental Host. (2020, September 8). *Which is harder to start and scale, rental arbitrage or co-hosting?* YouTube [Video] https://www. youtube.com/watch?v=scmRAbKvEPk

Short Term Sage - Airbnb, Vacation Rental Host. (2021, January 5). *Can you cohost with no prior hosting experience?* YouTube [Video] https://www.youtube.com/ watch?v=btP5nvX_gjc

STR University. (2017, January 7). *Airbnb hosting tips: TOP 5 THINGS I WISH I KNEW WHEN STARTING OUT!* YouTube [Video] https://www.youtube.com/ watch?v=A7Nvz8_ZFz0

STR University. (2018, May 25). *Should you get an LLC for your Airbnb?? (how to protect your assets).* YouTube [Video] https://www.youtube.com/watch?v=VRpu24vdcSQ

STR University. (2019, December 10). *3 marketing plat-forms all Airbnb hosts should be on in 2020!* YouTube [Video] https://www.youtube.com/watch?v= 9etT5OhEwtE

STR University. (2020a, February 11). *10 expert tips for new Airbnb hosts!* YouTube [Video] https://www. youtube.com/watch?v=HoHFGUcbpSU

STR University. (2020b, February 27). *Airbnb tax secrets: How to optimize your short term rental taxes with Clint Coons.* YouTube [Video] https://www.youtube.com/ watch?v=gQPcULVTnaM

Strangers Quotes. (n.d.). Famous Quotes. https://www. famousquotes123.com/strangers-quotes.html

Svetec, J. (2020a, June 16). *Airbnb management VS. co-hosting: What's the difference?* YouTube [Video] https:// www.youtube.com/watch?v=Y1euZG-tDro

Svetec, J. (2020b, June 23). *Understanding Airbnb regula-tions in your Area.* YouTube [Video] https://www. youtube.com/watch?v=hbkKeQeFtis

Svetec, J. (2020c, June 30). *Airbnb VS. HomeAway VS. Booking.com - Which one is BEST?* YouTube [Video]

https://www.youtube.com/watch?v=uyPTVGz2tng

Svetec, J. (2020d, December 10). *Airbnb VS. Booking.com VS. VRBO VS. HomeAway — What's the difference?* YouTube [Video] https://www.youtube.com/watch?v=y0SDL5gQMIo

Tax guidance for Airbnb hosts | Paying tax on Airbnb income. (2018). GoSimpleTax. https://www.gosimple tax.com/blog/airbnb-tax-guidance/

TED. (2016). How Airbnb designs for trust | Joe Gebbia YouTube [Video]. https://www.youtube.com/watch?v=16cM-RFid9U

The Business Channel. (2016). The real story about how Airbnb was founded - Nathan Blecharczyk Co-founder Airbnb - Startup Success YouTube [Video]. https://www.youtube.com/watch?v=M6GBqqk2mY4

The Fearless Investor. (2020, January 23). *4 ways to automate your AirBnB communication (SmartBnB Review).* YouTube [Video] https://www.youtube.com/watch?v=PqxUyQF-iIQ

The Fearless Investor. (2021a, March 25). *How to Co-*

Host on AirBnB. YouTube [Video] https://www.youtube.com/watch?v=i-jWmC3dGSg

The Fearless Investor. (2021b, December 9). *What does it mean to be a Co-Host on AirBnB?* YouTube [Video] https://www.youtube.com/watch?v=JyhIiVIN6ns

The Stuff I Use Channel. (2021). *How to get Airbnb tax 1099 forms.* YouTube [Video] https://www.youtube.com/watch?v=JPWr7vsrAYY

Top 5 things to consider before buying an Airbnb investment property. (n.d.). Carmichael Financial, LLC. https://carmichaelfinancial.net/articles/top-5-things-to-consider-before-buying-an-airbnb-investment-property

Vacation rental management software | Hospitable.com (ex Smartbnb). (2021, February 24). Hospitable. https://hospitable.com/

Vacation Rental School. (2020, January 24). *Booking.com vs. Airbnb in 2020.* YouTube [Video] https://www.youtube.com/watch?v=XVJecdsH1HE

What are the types of Airbnb guests? (2017, July 14). IGMS.

https://www.igms.com/6-types-of-vacation-rental-guests-and-how-to-attract-them/

What Co-Hosts can do - Airbnb Help Center. (n.d.). Airbnb. Retrieved May 10, 2022, from https://www.airbnb.co.za/help/article/1534/what-cohosts-can-do

What regulations apply to my city? - Airbnb Help Center. (n.d.). Airbnb. https://www.airbnb.co.za/help/article/961/what-regulations-apply-to-my-city?locale=en&_set_bev_on_new_domain=1651173858_NmVlMzY0MWM5YmQx

Whitmore, G. (2019, November 12). *8 pros and cons of staying in an Airbnb.* Forbes. https://www.forbes.com/sites/geoffwhitmore/2019/11/12/8-pros-and-cons-of-staying-in-an-airbnb/?sh=9989ead3c2f9

Why we require a profile - Airbnb Help Center. (n.d.). Airbnb. https://www.airbnb.co.za/help/article/67/why-we-require-a-profile?locale=en&_set_bev_on_new_domain=1651173858_NmVlMzY0MWM5YmQx

Zaragoza, R. (2021, November 26). *Conducting accurate Airbnb rental market analysis in 7 steps.* Investment Prop-

erty Tips | Mashvisor Real Estate Blog. https://www.
mashvisor.com/blog/airbnb-rental-market/

Ziraldo, K. (2022, April 22). *Airbnb investment: The pros
and cons*. Rocket Mortgage. https://www.rocketmort
gage.com/learn/airbnb-investment